THE

CRAFT BEER
DICTIONARY

An A–Z of craft beer,
from hop to glass

RICHARD CROASDALE

ILLUSTRATED BY JONNY HANNAH

MITCHELL BEAZLEY

CONTENTS

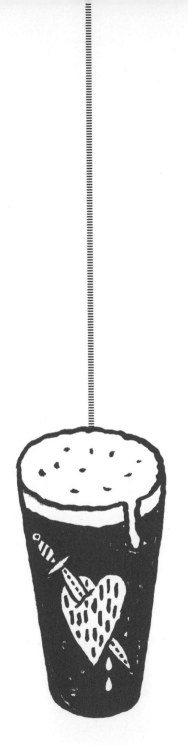

INTRODUCTION

Growing up in a sleepy English town, my formative booze years were in many ways a microcosm of the beer culture in Britain in the 1990s. Friday and Saturday nights were about Carlsberg, Heineken or, if you were feeling flush, Stella. At the other end of the scale, as the home of the Campaign for Real Ale's headquarters, we had plenty of cask-centric pubs dishing out their warm, flat pints to men who generally didn't take kindly to curious young drinkers.

Not really enjoying either experience, I simply decided beer wasn't for me and moved onto whisky, where I remained happily for the next decade.

It wasn't until the early 2000s that, having moved to Scotland, I discovered the delights of the well-brewed regional beers that are so common there. No doubt my palate had also improved since my Stella-swigging youth, but the subtle delights of Caledonian 80/- were something of an epiphany, and I set out to learn more. This was well timed, as the fruits of the American craft beer revolution were just beginning to arrive in Britain, first with Anchor's phenomenal Liberty Ale, then beers from the likes of Sierra Nevada, Founders and Stone. I was hooked, and have since taken every opportunity – professional and personal – to see the world's best beer regions for myself, meeting brewers, drinkers and pundits, in search of new flavours and fresh experiences.

Within this book, I have tried to capture some of that journey and alphabetize it. In the following pages, I'll outline the main process, techniques and pieces of equipment involved in brewing beer, both in a commercial brewery and at home (the two have a lot more in common than you might suspect). On the other side of the fence, I'll cover the basics of beer appreciation and culture, as well as what you should expect from some of the more common styles you will encounter as a curious beer lover.

None of this will give you a comprehensive "how-to"; you won't be able to brew a beer or run a bar after reading this book. But by dipping in, you should find it a ready reference for any unfamiliar terms or a source of more information on any beer-related topics that grab your attention.

Of course, it would be a little odd to attempt a craft beer dictionary without addressing the elephant in the room, and the most over-asked question in this multi-billion-dollar global industry: what is craft? In attempting an answer, most people will mention something about scale (small), ownership (independent), quality (good, obviously) and authenticity (we're basically sick of mass-produced "lager"). With this definition, though, the usual assumption that the craft "movement" began on the West Coast of America sounds a little less credible. After all, the brewing traditions of Europe – particularly Belgium, the UK and Germany – are undeniably rooted in ideas of craft, and have historically exhibited all the values of localism, quality and limited scale that are so prized by modern drinkers. Speak with today's craft brewers and you'll invariably find a huge respect for, and understanding of, these traditions. Far from seeing itself as a break from the past, the craft beer movement represents a rediscovery and evolution of the styles and techniques that were almost lost in the mid-20th century. For all their complaints about moustachioed, tattoo-festooned, bicycle-riding poseurs invading their pubs and disturbing their pints, traditional beer lovers have gained an army of comrades who (mostly) genuinely share their enthusiasm for quality and tradition.

So does this take us any closer to a definition? Having travelled the world meeting brewers ranging from garage enthusiasts and Belgian monks right through to the US craft behemoths, my somewhat woolly conclusion is that we generally know craft when we see it. Craft isn't about who paid for the brew kit, or how many barrels it churns out each year; it's in the passion of the people creating and brewing the beer. Most of all, though, craft is about the drinkers: their thirst for knowledge, for new sensations, for the latest and greatest. There is a palpable sense of excitement around beer today, and I for one hope that it never fades again.

ABV | BEER CULTURE

Alcohol by volume is a standardized, international measure of alcoholic strength, describing the amount of pure ethanol present in a solution, expressed as a percentage. Just to be confusing, there is an alternative way of expressing exactly the same thing in the US, where "alcohol proof" is simply twice the alcohol-by-volume number. For example, 42 percent ABV is 84 proof in the US.

ACETALDEHYDE | FAULT

A naturally occurring chemical common in ripe fruit, in beer acetaldehyde lends a tart, cider-like character reminiscent of green apples and is considered an off flavour. It is produced by yeast as an intermediate stage in the conversion of sugar into alcohol, and if the fermentation is not properly completed (that is, if the yeast for any reason is unable to finish the job) excess acetaldehyde can be left in the beer. Acetaldehyde can also occur when alcohol is exposed to oxygen – a particular problem with home-brew, where beer may be accidentally oxygenated after fermentation is complete. Further complications can occur if the beer is subsequently infected with certain strains of bacteria, which can convert acetaldehyde into acetic acid, whose sour vinegar character is even more offensive.

A

14

ACETOBACTER | SCIENCE

A bacterium that produces acetic acid in wine and beer, *Acetobacter* is rarely deliberately used in brewing – though it can be found in lambic, Flanders red ale and some wood-aged beers – because it consumes ethanol to produce this acid, which has a harsh character reminiscent of vinegar and pickle juices. *Acetobacter* requires a steady supply of oxygen to perform its fermentation.

ADJUNCT | INGREDIENT

Any grain, usually unmalted, used to supplement the main ingredient in the mash – almost always malted barley. Adjuncts are used for a number of reasons, from cutting costs with the inclusion of corn or rice (common in American light lagers) to adding desirable characteristics such as flavour, aroma, colour or texture. Many favourite craft styles, such as wheat beer, oatmeal stout and rye beer, use adjuncts as a key addition to the malt. Even styles in which an adjunct makes no obvious flavour contribution, such as IPA, may still use a small amount of wheat, for example, to improve head retention or create a smoother mouthfeel.

AGEING | HOME BREWING

With the right conditions, ageing beers at home is easy, fun and informative, as you get to observe the interesting changes that take place in them over time. The general rule is: dark, dry and cool (13–18°C/55–64°F), but some variation on that won't hurt – consistency of temperature is more important. Some of the most interesting effects are seen in bottle-conditioned ales and other beers where there is some residual macrobiotic

action. For example, in Belgian-style sour beers such as lambics, the sour complexity tends to intensify as the menagerie of hard-working yeast and bacteria keeps altering the chemical makeup of the beer. Strong, heavy ales – such as barley wines and imperial stouts – are the most common and satisfying candidates for ageing, though, as some of their rougher edges mellow into richer and more complex flavours. Most beers tend to dry out as they age and, as both sweetness and hop intensity drop, malt character and winey dark fruit notes can come to the fore. Ageing can also introduce some characteristics that would usually be considered off flavours, but that in the right context can add complementary notes. For example, oxidation can give dark beer sherry-like qualities, while autolysis adds savoury umami notes. These can go too far, though, and there's nothing more disappointing than opening a deliberately aged beer only to find it's past its best.

ALCOHOL | SCIENCE

The seemingly straightforward question of what alcohol actually is in the context of brewing turns out to be something of a Pandora's box. In beer circles, alcohol is largely synonymous with ethanol and, when alcohol by volume (ABV) is measured, it's really ethanol we're talking about. However, beer does contain tiny amounts of other alcohols, including methanol, propanol, iso-butanol and phenylethanol. While several of these ominously named "-nols" can be really quite bad for you if consumed in sufficient quantities (as can good old ethanol, to be fair), they can be useful on the flavour front, both in their own right and as precursors to other tasty compounds that form during fermentation. So-called "higher" or "fusel" alcohols – such as propanol, in particular – contribute a range of important flavours and are generally present at higher levels in ales than in "clean" lager beers. Once ingested, these fusel alcohols are metabolized into aldehydes, which are often stuck with the blame for painful hangovers. They can also be converted to delicious esters, which give beer lip-smacking fruit flavours, including pear, apple and apricot.

ALE | STYLES

SEE ALSO
Fermentation *p85*
Lager (definition 1) *p138*
Yeast *p243*

In beer taxonomy terms, ale is one of the two basic types of beer, the other being lager. Ale yeasts are almost always a strain of *Saccharomyces cerevisiae*, a top-fermenting brewer's yeast (in that it does its work near the top of the fermentation vessel) that thrives at higher temperatures than the bottom-fermenting yeasts used for lagers. As higher temperatures usually mean fermentation produces more flavour and aroma-imparting by-products, in addition to carbon dioxide and ethanol, ales have a stronger yeast influence in their character (and more intense flavours generally) than lagers.

ALPHA ACID | SCIENCE

SEE ALSO
Bitterness *p46*
Boil *p48*
Hops *p119*
Hops, bittering *p120*

Secreted by the lupulin glands of the hop cone, alpha acids are crucial to the flavour of most beers. When heated, usually during the boil phase of beer production, they form iso-alpha acids (a process called isomerization), which have a characteristic bitterness. The amount of alpha acids varies by hop variety, and is usually expressed as a percentage of the total dried weight of the hop cone. So, for example, a classic noble

hop such as Hallertau will have 2.5–5 percent alpha acids, while a New World variety such as Chinook could have up to 14 percent. As well as their flavour characteristics, iso-alpha acids also inhibit the growth of certain bacteria, which can spoil a brew. This preservative effect is thought to be the original reason for using hops in brewing.

AMBER ALE | STYLES

....

One of the first styles that a lot of craft converts will encounter, amber ales are different from your run-of-the-mill "big beer" offering, but not as challenging as a pale ale, for example. They typically don't have much in the way of aroma, though a medium dollop of bitterness helps balance the malt character, which should be the star of this particular show, with burnt sugar from the caramel malt and a touch of dried fruit.

AMERICA | ORIGIN

....

SEE ALSO
Adjunct *p14*
American lager *p20*

Aside from using hefty amounts of adjunct grains – primarily corn and rice – in its brews, the US doesn't really have much of a brewing tradition to draw upon. Never daunted, though, the Americans instead tended to adopt elements of everyone else's styles, techniques and hard-won knowledge and make something new and wonderful. From English IPAs with jacked-up ABV and juice-bomb American hops, to strong, complex Belgian-style *tripels*, there seems to be nothing to which American craft brewers can't turn their hand. Indeed, while the true craft of brewing was definitely born in Europe, it is in America that "craft brewing" originated as an idea and movement, without which it is unlikely we would be enjoying the current renaissance in regional styles and techniques.

AMERICAN IPA | STYLE

The American IPA takes the formula of the American pale ale and turns it up to 11, with more alcohol and a more in-your-face hop profile. The stakes have been raised still further over time, with the introduction of double IPAs (sometimes called DIPAs) and Imperial IPAs. So ubiquitous has this style become that several sub-styles now exist that are worthy of mention in their own right, as they have strayed pretty far from the original idea. West Coast IPAs are super-crisp and super-dry, with bags of hop aroma and negligible malt, whereas northeast IPAs (known as NEIPAs) are cloudy, soupy in mouthfeel, with a juicy hop profile and often luminous in colour.

AMERICAN LAGER | STYLE

The world's best-selling style of lager, using cheap, plentiful adjuncts – primarily rice and corn – to supplement the malt, usually to the tune of about 25 percent of the total mash bill. The price is inversely proportional to the quantity of adjuncts used, though few beers dare go beyond 50 percent. American lager's character is nondescript, with thin malt, the faintest whiff of bitterness and often a mouth-coating sweetness from the corn content. The current breed of adjunct lager emerged only in the late 19th century, and its march has long seemed unstoppable. Its offences pale into insignificance, however, alongside its dead-eyed and malevolent offspring: American light lager. This abomination was spawned in the 1940s and uses enzymes from fungus to convert all the carbohydrates present in the grain to fermentable sugar, resulting in a brew

with plenty of alcohol but fewer of the dreaded calories. Originally marketed as a diet beer for women, it was later branded "light" and sold to men, who bought it in their droves, to the point where it now outsells "fat" American lager. There is a tradition of sorts to all of this. Barley was scarce and valuable in the tough early years of America's history, whereas corn was easy to come by, so adjunct beer has been brewed there since the 16th century.

AMERICAN PALE ALE | STYLE

....

The quintessential American craft beer, and the style that started a global revolution. Drawing on traditional English pale ales and bitters, American pale ale (sometimes shortened to APA) is characterized by a pale golden malt base, with notes of caramel and raisin, balanced against those hallmark US hops, in all their piney, citrusy, floral glory. Though it's a strongly contested title, San Francisco brewery Anchor's Liberty Ale – launched way back in 1975 – probably has the best claim to being the original APA. This was followed five years later by Sierra Nevada and then by Blind Pig Brewery's Blind Pig Inaugural Ale. The original APAs struck a pretty even balance between malt and hops, although, as the hop craze has spread, subsequent entrants to this crowded category have leaned ever more heavily on that side of the scales.

SEE ALSO
American IPA *p20*
IPA *p128*
Pale ale *p165*

AROMA | TASTING

....

Aroma is a complex beast, and plays a much more active role in our experience of beer than one might suppose. For a start, our sense of smell essentially has a hotline to the parts of our brain responsible for emotion and long-

SEE ALSO
Essential oils *p81*
Hops *p119*
Hops, aroma *p120*

term memory – the faintest whiff of a familiar scent can be incredibly evocative of a particular time or place. Furthermore, it's a physiological fact that taste doesn't just take place on the tongue, a relatively crude sensory instrument; aromas released during the act of drinking and swallowing make their way onto two distinct sets of sensory receptors in the nasal cavity and are unconsciously blended with information from the tastebuds to form a more complex impression.

There are techniques to help you get the best out of nosing your beer. First, a good swirl really does help, as it coats the inside of the glass, giving volatile aromatic compounds the opportunity to be released. Give the contents a few good sharp sniffs (rather than one long breath), being sure to draw the air right into the top of your nasal cavity. Some tasters advocate taking in a little breath between the lips at the same time. The best tip for nosing beer, though (and wine, whisky or any other quality beverage you can think of), is simply practice. The more you consciously sample, the better you will become at picking out individual characteristics from the sensory riot and of making those deep associations with long-buried feelings and memories.

SEE ALSO
Bottles *p51*
Breweriana *p55*
Cans *p61*

ARTWORK | BEER CULTURE

Label and can artwork has long been an important part of the craft beer world, with many successful brands having developed their own distinctive and instantly recognizable style. This has been much to the chagrin of some beer traditionalists, who see eye-catching designs as a distraction from the important business of beer. Craft exponents would counter that they have elevated the humble can to a legitimate artistic

medium and that, if it bothers you that much, the beer tastes just as good with a paper bag wrapped around it. The refuseniks should, however, bear in mind that art and beer are old buddies. Long before Andy Warhol and his pop-art pals decided to take commercial design as their inspiration, Bass Ale's iconic red triangle became the UK's first registered trademark. That was in 1876; six years later it even made its way into a painting by Édouard Manet of the bar at the Folies-Bergères.

ATTENUATION | SCIENCE

The percentage of sugar that a yeast is expected to convert to alcohol, carbon dioxide and flavour compounds. This varies depending on the strain of yeast, the fermentation conditions and the gravity of the particular beer being brewed, and is a key part of the brewer's calculations. For example, many Belgian yeasts, as well as those used for the popular West Coast IPA style, employ high-attenuation yeasts to achieve their characteristically dry flavour profile. An English-style mild ale, on the other hand, would call for a yeast strain that does not attenuate as much, leaving more of the sugar unfermented and giving a slightly lower ABV. By understanding the expected attenuation of a particular yeast strain in a particular beer, brewers can use gravity readings to confirm whether fermentation has completed successfully. The typical attenuation range for brewer's yeasts is between 65 and 85 percent.

AUTOLYSIS | SCIENCE

The root cause of a common off flavour, particularly in old beers, occurring when yeast cells die, rupture and disgorge their contents into the beer, autolysis is characterized by a savoury, soy sauce or even burnt rubber flavour and aroma. In small amounts, however, it can add interesting depth to aged beers – particularly rich, dark styles – and is the same chemical process that gives some champagnes their characteristic toasty notes. It can be caused by excess stress being placed on the yeast during fermentation – for example excessively rapid temperature changes (stressed and unhappy yeast cells are generally more prone to autolysis) – or simply by leaving dead yeast resting in the fermented beer.

BACTERIA | SCIENCE

SEE ALSO
Acetobacter p14
Cleaning p66
Lactobacillus p137
Pediococcus p166
Sour p207

Whether introduced deliberately or through carelessness, the presence of bacteria during fermentation can have a dramatic effect. Like yeast, these bugs love the sugar in wort, but instead of alcohol their primary product is acid (the type of acid depends on the bacteria). In most styles and traditions, the sourness resulting from a bacterial infection is considered a major flaw, though in some it is a vital part of a beer's character. When introduced deliberately, bacteria are either added in a controlled way, from a pure source, or allowed to infect the beer through the environment (from the air or the surface of the fermentation vessel). Bacteria are hardy beasts, so breweries must maintain a rigorous cleaning programme to avoid unwanted infection. Particular care must be taken when a brewer has made an intentionally sour beer, then switched back to conventional yeast-only fermentation. The same is true in pubs and bars, where bacteria can linger in tap lines unless they are properly cleaned (or replaced).

BALANCE | TASTING

SEE ALSO
Carbonation *p62*
Hops *p119*

The interplay between the various flavour components (primarily sweet malt and bitter hops) in a beer. While most beer styles lean slightly more heavily to either the malt or the hop side, these two broad tastes are complementary and should work in harmony. This judgment is largely subjective and, while the give and take of sweetness and bitterness are the main factors in the balance equation, there are many other potential influences, including acidity, the roast level of the malt and the level of carbonation.

BARLEY | INGREDIENT

Barley (*Hordeum vulgare*, to give it its Latin name) is one of the world's oldest cultivated grains, having been grown in agriculture for 13,000 years. It has a rich, nutty flavour, deliciously chewy consistency and its high concentrations of the sugar maltose make it great for sustenance. In ancient Greece and Egypt it was often used to make cheap bread, but in the process it was found it was ideal for brewing. Technically a member of the grass family, barley is tall and thin in the wild, with several spikes on top from where the grains come.

When barley is malted it produces enzymes that release the tasty sugars stored deep inside. These are normally used by the plant to fuel the explosive growth of its seed, but if the germination process is halted prematurely, the sugar is available for us to use in basic sweets, flavoured drinks or fermentation. Today, around 150 million tons of barley are produced every year. Modern, farmed barley is quite different from the wild barley of Babylonian times, as farmers have selectively bred for useful characteristics. It comes in two main types: two-row and six-row. Two-row, the original type, has grains growing only from the plant's central spike, either side, in two rows, and is low in protein. Six-row barley is another genetic

mutation, in which grains grow from three spikes, giving six rows. It is high in protein and enzymes, which can cause troublesome cloudiness, but produces a higher yield, so is more economical. Barley is not only the fundamental sugar source for brewing; it also contributes colour, flavours and textures. Malted barley is dried and then sometimes roasted after germination – a key factor in the flavour it contributes. While other grains are often found in brewing, malted barley remains the star for several important reasons. For one thing, it contains useful husks, which protect the grains from handling, keep the mash loose and form a filter during lautering. It's also much easier to malt than wheat and has a lower protein content, plus it's cheap and easy to grow. Finally, in its pale form it has a very neutral character, which allows brewers to have more control over their final product (by adding character with other modified grains such as oats, rice or corn) and create the delicious range of beers we've all come to love.

BARLEY WINE | STYLE

SEE ALSO
Barrel-ageing p34
Wee heavy p232

One of only a small handful of very strong English ales, barley wine is an old rural style, traditionally brewed for the winter months. The first commercial barley wine labelled as such was the "No. 1 strong ale" released by Bass at the start of the 20th century. It's similar in character to a Scottish wee heavy, though usually somewhat lighter in colour and with a more pronounced hop character to balance out its intense malty sweetness. Its aroma is rich and fruity, complemented by spice from noble hops, to give a distinctly Christmassy feel. Often barrel-aged for extra layers of character.

BARREL-AGEING | BREWING

Wooden barrels have been at the heart of alcohol making for literally millennia, and the skill of the cooper (barrel-maker) revered for just as long. For all brown spirits, the majority of the flavours you enjoy come out of the complex chemistry and fibrous flesh of the woods in which they were aged. Many wines, too, owe a significant amount of their character to the barrel; it's not just a convenient vessel for storage. In most cases, this wood will have come from an oak tree – generally *Quercus alba* in America, *Quercus robur* in Europe – prized for both its flavour and its ability to provide an almost watertight seal against the environment.

The fact that it's an *almost* watertight seal is important, though. Oak is slightly porous and, as such, will absorb some of the character of whatever is stored in it, even as it leaches out its own woody flavours – a process that is helped along by any changes in air pressure and temperature, which effectively pump the liquid in and out of the porous surface. For brewers, who tend to reuse barrels previously employed for another alcohol – whether bourbon, Scotch whisky, wine or a plethora of others – this interaction between the beer, the barrel and its previous occupant is a treasure-trove of flavours and aromas. But barrel-ageing isn't just about adding external flavours to the beer. There is complex chemistry taking place inside that quiet vessel as compounds combine, break down and mature into more complex flavour and aroma congeners: chemistry that even whisky-makers – for whom barrels are day-to-day apparatus – are only just beginning to understand. Some styles of beer are obviously more suited to barrel-ageing than others – a

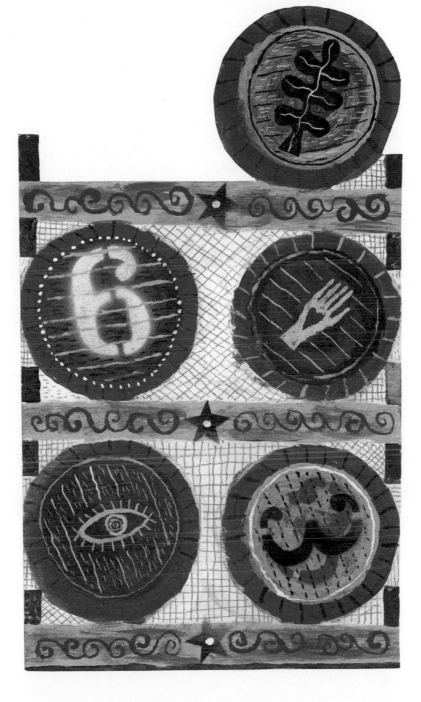

strong Imperial stout or barley wine, for example, will stand up to wood influence rather better than a crisp, refreshing pilsner.

BEARD | BEER CULTURE

Facial hair is ubiquitous in craft beer circles, at least among the male contingent. Design is down to the taste and conscience of the individual drinker, though beard length often correlates to one's place in the scene's strict social hierarchy. Beards are not just useful for identification and decoration, though: Oregon's Rogue Ales "Beard Beer" is brewed using a culture isolated from head brewer John Maier's own face furniture. It is surprisingly tasty.

BEER BELLY | DRINKING

While beer doesn't have any special properties that guarantee the characteristic pot belly, it is a major source of calories and, as such, will make you fat if you drink it in excess (obviously). Beer contains carbohydrates and several kinds of sugar, while alcohol – which is itself a sugar – hides away roughly seven calories per gram, making it as calorific as pure fat. Consequently, stouts and ales can clock in at around 250 calories a pint – a good chunk of your recommended daily allowance. As an extra treat, alcohol stimulates the appetite, making you more susceptible to over-eating: another good reason to intersperse your drinking with glasses of water.

BEER FEAR | DRINKING

SEE ALSO
Drunkenness *p77*
Hangover *p109*

We've all been there. It's 3am and you're suddenly, startlingly awake from your cuddly, beer-induced slumber. The drink that reassured you earlier that everything was (and would always be) fine is now giving you a quite different message: you embarrassed yourself tonight, everyone thought you were a dullard, and you've quite probably left your phone in a toilet.

My friend, that's the beer fear talking. Alcohol is a well-known depressant, acting on your brain in a number of ways, from depleting its favourite nutrients and drying it out to triggering certain hormonal reactions. Add that to the rather unpleasant physical symptoms of being hungover – pain, nausea, dizziness – and it's hard not to conclude that there's something terribly wrong with the world.

SEE ALSO
Germany *p99*
Oktoberfest *p162*

BEER HALL | DRINKING

A particular style of pub, originating in the Bavarian capital of Munich, but now found throughout Germany and across the world (particularly in those parts of the US that took in a large number of German migrant labourers during the late 19th and early 20th centuries). Beer halls tend to be extremely large, high-ceilinged affairs, typically seating several hundred people (though sometimes thousands) on long, communal benches. Most belong to a particular brewery, or even have a microbrewery on site, and serve a limited range of traditional beer styles, along with traditional Bavarian food.

SEE ALSO
Drunkenness *p77*

BEER JACKET | DRINKING

You know it's a cold night but somehow, after a few beers, it doesn't seem quite so bad – you've donned your warming beer jacket. It's a real thing, but it doesn't work the way you think. One of the first effects of consuming alcohol is a widening of the tiny capillary blood vessels all

over your body, giving you a feeling of warmth, particularly in your extremities. However, while sending warm blood to those areas of your body most prone to losing heat may feel good, it will actually lead to a lowering of your core temperature. So, if you're really cold, steer clear of the beer.

SEE ALSO
Artwork *p24*
Breweriana *p55*

BEER MATS | DRINKING

Card beer mats or coasters were one of the first forms of commercial beer advertising, originating in Germany in the 1880s before catching on globally around 40 years later. Around 5.5 billion beer mats are manufactured annually, and the international market is dominated by just two companies. Designed to soak up slops, beer mats are inherently disposable, yet some are also collectable. Tegestology (from the Latin *teges*, meaning a reed mat) is the hobby of collecting beer mats and is taken very seriously by its adherents, with swap meets, internet forums and auction sites dedicated to trading and sharing information about mats old and new.

BEER PONG | DRINKING

A classic US drinking game, thought to have originated in the 1950s in Dartmouth College, New Hampshire. Usually played in two teams, it involves throwing ping-pong balls along a table into a row of cups of beer lined up in front of the opposing team. Each time a ball lands in a cup (known as a "make"), the opposing team is obliged to drink its contents. If you play this game with craft beer, you don't deserve to have nice things.

SEE ALSO
Esters *p82*
Pilsner *p170*

BELGIAN BLONDE | STYLE

Belgium's ale-based answer to the scourge of light pilsners. Leaning firmly to the malt side of the balance, this easy-drinking light ale emerged in the 1920s and is delicately malty, with sweet caramel notes, background hop bitterness and a classic fruity, estery Belgian yeast.

SEE ALSO
Tripel p224

BELGIAN GOLDEN ALE | STYLE

Sharing a lot of characteristics with the monastic *tripel*, Belgian golden ales such as Duvel and Delirium Tremens pack quite a punch, in terms of both alcoholic strength (up to around 11 percent) and flavour/aroma. The malt is pronounced but very crisp, with a clean, noble-hop bitterness working exceptionally well with a bone-dry body and spicy yeast profile.

SEE ALSO
Phenols *p169*
Trappist *p223*

BELGIUM | ORIGIN

The diminutive northern European country that is the butt of so many ignorant jokes, yet home to some of the greatest beers, brewers and bars anywhere. In a nutshell, the Belgians have been at it since the Iron Age and, while their beer shares a lot of roots with the great British and German brewing traditions, it is so distinctive (and occasionally so downright weird) that it makes the rest of the beer world look positively homogenous. From the great flat farmlands of Flanders to the lofts of Brussels and the potent holy brews of Trappist monks, Belgium's unique blend of tradition, innovation, craft, mysticism and practicality has produced many beers that transcend "style" as most of us understand it. The result is an awful lot of beers that don't really conform, brewed using different ingredients –

including unconventional grains, fruit, exotic spices and more – and a whole range of unique techniques to achieve a particular result. At the heart of all this, though, is the one factor that Belgian beer is perhaps best known for: yeast. Where British and American brewers have historically used only a handful of yeasts (and German lagers basically stick to two), Belgium is a true yeast-lover's sweetshop. Even leaving aside the exotic wild critters found in lambics, the character of Belgian yeasts ranges from lip-smackingly fruity right through Middle-Eastern spicy to sharply phenolic.

BERLINER WEISSE | STYLE

SEE ALSO
Lactobacillus p137
Sour p207

A great style that's had a rough ride over the past century or so, with steadily declining production and an apparent destiny as a low-rent regional attraction in Berlin's more touristy beer bars. The noisome practice of serving *Berliner weisse* with a shot of raspberry syrup or essence of woodruff seems finally to be falling out of favour, though, as a new generation of craft beer lovers in Berlin and beyond wake up to its simple charms. Unadulterated, it's a refreshing, low-alcohol brew whose clean, yogurty tartness is a brilliant quencher on a hot day. It's a kettle sour, so fairly quick to brew and pretty accessible for the sour newbie. It also takes fruit additions very well, and its US-led craft resurgence has been a veritable fruit salad of passionfruit, grapefruit, peach and (in a nod to its recent inauspicious history) even raspberry.

BEST BEFORE | BEER CULTURE

SEE ALSO
Ageing *p14*
Off flavours *p161*
Oxidation *p164*

While beers are required to carry a "best before" date in many markets, it is not really the same as the date on a raw chicken, for example. As beer is naturally hostile to any microbial spoilage, you won't get sick from drinking an out-of-date brew (whereas eating a chicken that's been ageing in your basement for years probably isn't the best idea). Instead, the "best before" date on beer is an indication of when the brewer believes its flavour, aroma, mouthfeel and so on will have broken down to the point that the beer should no longer be considered a good representation of its kind. Given the right conditions, however, some beers can be aged far beyond their "best before" date, and their character will change over time – in a sense, these beers are going "off" in a good way. Some breweries have even started including "best after" dates on their bottles, indicating that the beer should be left for a time before it is ready to drink. This seems a little like cheating.

BITTERNESS | STYLE

To a greater or lesser extent a key part of the character profile of most beers, bitterness is most commonly associated with hops, though can also come from dark, roasted malts and from additives such as coffee. Although there are semi-objective ways of measuring it, perceived bitterness is an altogether more complicated beast, affected by sweetness, malt character, temperature and even carbonation. For example, most stouts and porters are objectively higher in bitterness than even the gnarliest hop-forward IPA, yet their sweetness and body make it much less noticeable.

BLENDING | BREWING

Batches of beer are often combined to reach a target flavour profile. The term "blending" is mostly associated with barrel-aged or

SEE ALSO
Alpha acid *p17*
Balance *p29*
Hops, bittering *p120*

SEE ALSO
Barrel-ageing *p34*
Foeder *p96*
Sour *p207*
Spontaneous fermentation
 p208

spontaneously fermented beers. The beer to be blended can be a mix of old and new, have spent time in barrels or foeders or can even have been steeped with fruit – the master blender must have a grip on all of this, and must select each source at precisely the right moment of readiness and bring them together to create something delicious that has both nuance and balance.

BOCK | STYLE

Reputedly originating in the German town of Einbeck, *bock* is a strong lager, with several sub-styles ranging in colour from the light *maibock* or *heller bock* to the deep reddish-brown *dunkel bock*. All variations tend to have a rich, sweet malt profile, barely offset by hops, and a full, satisfying body. The *dunkel* (dark) *bock* has a toasted, biscuit malt quality with hints of caramel chocolate, while the lighter *maibock* has an equally rich but less toasty caramel malt.

There also exist two much stronger *bock* variations: *doppelbock* (or double *bock*) and *eisbock* (or ice *bock*). The former is simply brewed with a higher original gravity and even more strident malt profile, while *eisbock* is partially frozen after fermentation in order to remove some of its water content and concentrate the alcohol, which can go up to 14 percent ABV.

BODY | TASTING

The perceived weight or thickness of a beer. This is influenced by a number of factors, such as the type and concentration of grain proteins, sweetness, the attenuation of the yeast (dryness) and, to an extent, carbonation.

SEE ALSO
Attenuation *p27*
Fermentation *p85*
Mouthfeel *p155*

BOIL | BREWING

After mashing and sparging have extracted everything useful from the grain, the resulting wort is ready to be boiled. Boiling is a crucial and surprisingly complex part of the brewing process, bringing about a host of important chemical changes. As well as halting the enzyme action from the mash, it also sterilizes any unwanted bugs in the wort, removes certain volatile compounds that could otherwise cause off flavours, isomerizes the alpha acids from hops, reduces the volume of the wort, thereby concentrating it, and causes unwanted proteins to clump together and drop out (a process known as the "hot break"). During the boil, hops are often added in several stages. Those added at the start will achieve the most isomerization, but also lose the most of their aromatic essential oils through evaporation. Brewers may choose to make further "flavour additions", adding hops toward the end of the boil to extract a mix of bitterness and aroma. Hops may also be added after the boil for pure aroma. It's important that the boil is just that: a strong rolling boil that keeps the wort at 100°C (212°F) for the full 60–90 minutes. The volume lost during this time depends on the shape and configuration of the kettle, and experienced brewers will know their kit and adjust their boiling times and volumes accordingly.

BOIL KETTLE | EQUIPMENT

The boil kettle, or copper as it is sometimes known, is the vessel to which the wort is transferred after mashing. Kettles must have a powerful heat source to bring the wort up to boiling point as quickly as possible and keep it there for an hour or more. Boil kettles would

originally have been heated with direct flame, though this had several drawbacks, including lack of control and a tendency to burn the sugars in the wort. Most modern kettles use either a slightly modified direct fire arrangement, an electric heating element (which is the norm in home-brewing) or a low-pressure gas-fired steam heater. Each of these has its advantages and disadvantages, depending on the scale of the brewery and the amount of flexibility it needs to produce different styles. Again depending on the size of the brewery, the kettle may also incorporate a whirlpool to help separate the hot break from the wort before cooling. In larger breweries, the whirlpool is a separate vessel.

SEE ALSO
Cocktails *p66*
Scottish ales *p194*

BOILERMAKER | DRINKING

....

A classic US serve, consisting of a pint of ale accompanied by a single shot glass of bourbon. Traditionally, the bourbon is knocked back and then chased by the beer, which is drunk in sips. Some prefer to "bomb" the bourbon into the pint, though this is arguably a waste of both. Many other cultures have their equivalent serve. In Scotland, the half-and-half (or hauf-n-hauf) is a popular way of drinking whisky, a dram being served with half a pint of Scottish ale (a medium 80/- works best). In Holland, *Jenever* (a gin-like spirit) is paired with beer to make *Kopstootje* (literally translated as "a little headbutt"), and in Germany, *Korn* (a kind of grain brandy) is served alongside beer for a *Herrengedeck* (literally, and ominously, a "gentleman's menu").

SEE ALSO
Glassware *p99*
Light strike *p143*
Oxidation *p164*

BOTTLES | EQUIPMENT

....

Glass bottles are deeply engrained in our beer culture, to the point where we almost fetishize them. And rightly so; after all, if the histories are true, in some parts of the world we've been drinking out of them for at least 400 years. The earliest bottles were fragile, irregular and prone to exploding under the pressure of carbon dioxide buildup. They were also, ironically, the object of considerable scorn from ale purists, who complained they tainted the brew. With innovations such as glass moulds, crown caps and screw tops, bottles gradually became a more convenient and cost-effective option. Surprisingly, though, they remained a fairly niche product until the early 20th century, and their rapid growth in popularity peaked at the start of the 1960s, before keg and can began to erode their share. Today, glass bottles come in a variety of shapes and sizes, depending on their country of origin and the style of beer. Though the Industry Standard Bottle (ISB) or North American Longneck dominates, in 330ml and 500ml sizes, Belgian brewers frequently use squat 330ml *steinies* or tall elegant champagne-style bottles, while many German beers come in tapering NRW (Nord-Rhein Westfalen) bottles. So, although they're fragile, difficult to transport, terrible to drink from and not even particularly good at protecting their contents, bottles are pretty and make us feel as if we're upholding a tradition, so they will probably be around for a while yet.

BRETTANOMYCES | SCIENCE

Translating literally as "British yeast", *Brettanomyces* – or "brett" – is actually more commonly associated with Belgian brewing and styles such as lambic, *gueuze* and some *saisons*. It's an acquired taste and produces what would be considered off flavours in most beer styles. Its

characteristic flavours and aromas are variously described as funky, straw and wet horse blanket. Although brett is typically used alongside conventional strains of *Saccharomyces* brewer's yeast, some brewers do their fermentation with 100 percent brett. It is found in sour beer styles such as lambic and Flanders Red, but does not itself produce any significant sour flavours – a common misconception. Instead, it is frequently used alongside souring bacteria, such as *Lactobacillus* and *Pediococcus*, to enhance depth and complexity.

BREWERIANA | BEER CULTURE

Beer has always had a lot of material knick-knacks associated with it. In craft beer, we tend to call it "merch" – after all, beer is the new rock and roll, don't you know? This stuff has been around for a very long time, though, with some examples dating back to the Victorian era. Examples include beer mats and towels, pump clips, trays, advertising, bottle openers, bottle caps, labels, ceramic ornaments, glassware mirrors and countless other promotional items. The fundamental rule of breweriana is: if it's reasonably old and can be associated with a beer or brewery, someone out there will want to buy it. Just look online if you're sceptical. Keen collectors often focus on a particular type of item, region or even brewery in their search, and will pay very serious money for a rare and long-sought specimen.

BREWHOUSE | EQUIPMENT

The collective term for all the various pieces of equipment used to brew beer (usually excluding the fermentation vessels), as well as the building in which the wort is brewed. Brewhouse capacity is usually measured in barrels (or "bbl"), with most craft breweries using a two-, three- or four-vessel brewhouse. In a two-vessel system, mash tun and later tun are combined, as are the boil kettle and whirlpool. With three-vessels, one of these combined vessels is separated out, while in a four-vessel system, each function has its own separate container. More vessels generally mean more flexibility and higher overall capacity. Some very large craft breweries have five or even six vessels, including a wort receiver and a hop strainer.

BREWPUB | DRINKING

SEE ALSO
Taproom p219

If a taproom is a brewery with a bar attached, a brewpub is a bar with a brewery attached. Brewpubs go back centuries – predating modern commercial breweries – but became popular again in America as the appetite for locally brewed beer of provenance began to grow. Brewpubs will often make a feature of their fermentation tanks and brewhouse, enclosing them in a glassed-off section so that customers can feel part of the fun.

BRITAIN | ORIGIN

SEE ALSO
CAMRA p61
Cask p65
Pub p177
Real ale p184

Britain's brewing history dates back 5,000 years, give or take, and anthropologists believe the tradition in this island nation sprang up on its own, without any influence or knowledge imported from overseas. Of course, over the millennia Brits have imported and incorporated know-how through trade and invasion, from everyone from the Romans to the Flemish (whom we have to thank for the introduction of hops in the 14th century). Traditional British styles

tend to be soft, mild and relatively low in alcohol, well balanced with complex malt character and a touch of European hop bitterness. Real ale is the jewel in Britain's beer crown, though. These complex, cask-conditioned, gently sparkling ales are Britain's alone and, while they came close to being wiped out by the march of foreign lagers, have found a new, young and appreciative audience among the craft beer crowd, who have rediscovered their subtle and sophisticated delights. Britain also has its own unique drinking culture, based around the traditional pub, a true national institution and – historically at least – a hub for community, commerce and politics. Pubs, too, have been under threat for decades, though once again craft is helping turn this around.

SEE ALSO
Aroma *p23*
Pale ale *p165*

BROWN ALE | STYLE

A beer that had been around in England since time immemorial before anyone bothered to try to define it. It's not the most exciting style in the world, but can have its own subtle, gentle beauty if done well. Lacking the hoppy kick of an English bitter or pale ale, its malt character really shines, though, with a complex, nutty aroma, a soft, toasty palate and a touch of caramel. Brown ale has recently been rediscovered by some breweries at the more traditional, cask-oriented end of the UK craft scene, as well as by American brewers with a respect for "Old World" brewing sensibilities.

CAMRA | BEER CULTURE

The Campaign for Real Ale, established in 1971 to combat the perceived threat of macro-brewing – specifically lager – to Britain's real-ale brewing tradition. It holds events across the UK, from huge beer festivals to tiny local tastings, and is as much a forum for discussion as a means of discovering new ales. It is also an organized and passionate advocate for British pubs and brewing in local and national government, and its campaigns have been behind many beer-friendly legislative changes over the past 45 years. Since the rise of craft beer in the UK, the organization has sought to modernize and ensure its relevance to a new generation of beer lovers.

CANS | EQUIPMENT

Depending on where you are in the world and who you happen to be talking to, cans are either the ideal vessel for transporting and storing single servings of beer or a metallic embodiment of everything that's wrong with modern "craft" beer. Lined with an inert plastic, today's cans are not susceptible to metal contamination (a common complaint aimed at their forebears). They also don't let in any light, keeping all-important hop compounds safe from UV damage; they chill more rapidly and are much more space-efficient than bottles, helping keep shipping costs down. Beer was first sold in cans in 1935, using an odd, conical design that tapered to a traditional bottle cap. Interestingly, the first non-US brewery to adopt the technology was the tiny Felinfoel Brewery in Wales; examples of the Felinfoel pale ale can now sell at auction for more than £1,400 ($1,900). Basic can design has not changed dramatically for decades, though "360-degree" cans – from which the entire lid can be removed, supposedly for better nosing – are becoming increasingly common.

CARBONATION | SCIENCE

A natural by-product of fermentation, carbon dioxide gas dissolves easily in water-based liquids, and a pint of cold beer can hold a surprising amount of it. As beer warms or is released from a pressurized vessel such as a keg or can, the dissolved gas begins to coalesce, eventually producing bubbles that rise to the surface, forming a head. Purists will tell you the only correct way to carbonate a beer is through natural conditioning in a cask or bottle. However, many beers – even your favourite craft brews – will have been force-carbonated: the gas is pumped into the flat beer under pressure until the correct amount has been dissolved. Forced carbonation is much easier to control and there is little sensory or scientific evidence to suggest natural carbonation gives a different character of bubble. Not all beers are carbonated equally, and good brewers will vary their carbonation according to style. British-style cask ales suit low carbonation, not least because they are served relatively warm. Styles such as lagers or pilsners, best served cold, tend to be more heavily carbonated for a lively, refreshing mouthfeel.

CASK | STYLE

Cask beer is unfiltered, unpasteurized and
undergoes a secondary fermentation inside
a cask, to be served without the addition of
carbon dioxide or nitrogen. Subtle, rounded
and naturally effervescent (generally less
bubbly than kegged beer), cask ales are a
distinctly British phenomenon and a source of
fierce pride for a certain subset of UK beer lovers.
Rather than being chilled like keg beers, most
cask ales are served at "cellar temperature",
which is generally considered to be 11–13°C
(52–55°F). Because of the "live" nature of
cask ales, they tend to be more sensitive to
mistreatment, and storing and serving cask
is considered something of an art form. Pubs
that have been audited and found to have the
necessary setup and skills may be awarded a
"Cask Marque" badge of quality.

CICERONE | BEER CULTURE

Irked by the fact that beer had no recognized
equivalent of a wine sommelier, craft beer
expert Ray Daniels set up the Cicerone
Certification Programme in 2007. Starting out
in the US, the programme has since expanded
internationally and is now seen as the gold
standard for bartenders, consultants, pundits
and even ordinary beer lovers looking to prove
their mettle. The certification framework has
four levels, ranging from Certified Beer Server
at level one through to Master Cicerone at level
four. Depending on the level, examinations
cover topics including style, correct serving
techniques and food pairing, as well as essays
and in-depth sensory tests.

CLEANING | BREWING

There is an old maxim that brewing is about 90 percent cleaning. If anything, this overstates the glamour of the job, as the level of hygiene at every stage of the process must be meticulous. Anyone who's attempted to brew beer at home will know how badly wrong things can go if even the smallest amount of wild bacteria or foreign yeast gets into fermenting beer; it can ruin the entire batch. Scale this up and consider the number of opportunities that exist for infection in a large, busy brewery, and you begin to understand why even the best, most gifted and creative brewers spend a lot of time with a power-washer in their hands, worrying about sugary deposits in hoses.

COCKTAILS | DRINKING

Beer cocktails divide popular opinion between those who believe they are a work of pure, unremitting evil and those who enjoy drinking works of pure unremitting evil. From a simple shandy through to lavish creations involving whisky and shaved tonka beans, beer cocktails have undeniably enjoyed a resurgence in recent years, as juicy, hop-forward styles have given mixologists a new palate of tropical fruit characteristics to play with.

COLD BREAK | BREWING

Following the boil, the wort is rapidly chilled down to a temperature where the yeast can safely be pitched. This sudden temperature drop also causes various proteins, carbohydrates and oils to stick together and precipitate from the wort; the resulting goop is the cold break, and can safely be removed. This is an important

step in the brewing process, as these chemicals can cause chill haze if left in the wort, and slower cooling increases the opportunities for unwanted infection.

COLOUR | TASTING

SEE ALSO
Maillard browning *p145*
Malting *p146*

It is true that we taste with our eyes before a pint touches our lips, so colour – and the expectations it gives us – is hugely important, and brewers take it very seriously. Although beer exists in many shades and hues, the universally accepted way of measuring it is a single scale from light to dark, ranging from the very palest straw right through to completely opaque. As most beer is reddish-yellow in colour, it is most opaque to blue light, so this is used to measure its optical density, on a piece of specialized equipment called a spectrophotometer. Brilliantly (and there are no points for spotting a pattern here) the US and Europe use different scales for measuring precisely the same thing in precisely the same way. In the US, the Standard Reference Method (SRM) is laid down by the American Society of Brewing Chemists (ASBC) and runs from the palest straw at two, to black at 40-plus. In Europe, the European Brewery Convention (EBC) reigns, with black around 80. For easy conversion (with caveats, of course), EBC ratings are roughly double their SRM equivalent.

COMPETITIONS | BEER CULTURE

SEE ALSO
Colour *p69*
Home-brew *p113*
Style *p216*

Whether you are a home-brewer or a seasoned professional, competitions offer a great opportunity to test your skills and creativity on a (supposedly) impartial audience. Beer competitions tend to be obsessive about style, and no beer, however closely it fulfils the brewer's intention, will get a look-in if it isn't "to style". The exact parameters of any given style include expectations for flavour, aroma and texture, as well as colour measured on the SRM or EBC scale and a rough figure for alcoholic strength, all set out in a number of standardized guides, such as that from the Beer Judge Certification Programme (BJCP) and the American Home-brew Association (AHA). Some of the more common styles are outlined elsewhere in this book. Competitions are strictly egalitarian; age, gender and background are no obstacle to success, and many a professional brewing career has started with a pimply teen confounding older peers by striking gold with a garage brew. They're also great social events, where you can mix with other brewers, get feedback and share tips.

CONDITIONING | BREWING

SEE ALSO
Carbonation *p62*
Cask *p65*
Fermentation *p85*
Secondary fermentation
 p198

A vital step in many beers, occurring at the end of fermentation. The remaining yeast in suspension is given a final burst of activity, often with the addition of a small amount of priming sugar, to create further carbon dioxide (sometimes referred to as "condition"). This is then dissolved in the beer, rather than being vented into the air, as is the case during primary fermentation. Conditioning can happen in the bottle or the cask, and some breweries are even experimenting with can-conditioning.

COOLING | BREWING

SEE ALSO
Boil *p48*
Cold break *p66*
Coolship *p71*
DMS *p74*
Off flavours *p161*
Wort *p240*

In brewing, after the wort is boiled, it is cooled rapidly to halt ongoing chemical reactions and reduce the risk of microbial infection. Cooling is achieved in a number of ways, usually depending on the scale of the brewery. In home-brew, it often involves a simple heat exchanger, in which the hot wort is run through a long, narrow tube either submerged in cold water or encased in a slightly wider tube through which cold water is constantly flowing. The beer is cooled as the surrounding water is warmed. For very small brewkits, an immersion chiller may be used, which cools the wort in situ. Most craft breweries of any size will use a more sophisticated glycol cooling system, which works in a broadly similar way to your refrigerator at home, but on a much larger scale. Some will even capture the heat from cooling wort and use it to warm the mash in the next brew.

COOLSHIP | EQUIPMENT

A coolship (or *koelship*, in the original, unanglicized Flemish) is a broad, flat, shallow open fermentation vessel, traditionally used to cool hot wort rapidly. Because they're open to the environment, coolships are frequently used in spontaneously fermented beers, where the yeasts and other microorganisms present in the air infect the wort and give the resulting fermentation a unique character. Coolships are perhaps most closely associated with Belgian lambics and their most famous proponent, Cantillon of Brussels. However, they also have a long history in the US (San Francisco "steam" beers reputedly take their name from the steaming rooftop coolships historically used in that city), with Anchor Brewing Company and Maine's Allagash keeping their use alive.

CORN | INGREDIENT

Corn (maize) is a cheap and plentiful source of fermentable sugars in beer, and is often associated with the relatively flavourless mass-market lagers that have dominated since the 1970s. However, the judicious use of corn as an adjunct is not always a bad thing: it can add desirable characteristics to both lagers and ales, including a smooth, light sweetness. Before it can be added to the mash, corn must be gelatinized by boiling, in order to break down its longer starches. Corn for brewing comes in many forms, including malted corn, cornmeal, corn grits, flaked maize and even dextrose (which is essentially corn sugar). It should be kept to a relatively small proportion of the mash bill, as too much can cause cider or solvent off flavours in the finished beer.

CORNELIUS KEG | EQUIPMENT

Originally used in soft-drink distribution, the Cornelius (or "Corney") keg has been enthusiastically adopted by home-brewers as a relatively cheap and convenient way of achieving the draft experience for their brews. Unlike a standard keg, which has a single opening and requires a special filling station, a Cornelius keg has three openings: one for filling, one for draft gas in and one for liquid out. It's a wonderfully simple design that, with some basic understanding of how draft systems work, is pretty tricky to mess up.

SEE ALSO
American IPA *p20*
Hops *p119*

DANK | FAULT

You'll sometimes hear beers with a super-pungent, resinous hop profile referred to as "dank". Given that this style of beer was popularized in California, it is perhaps unsurprising to learn that the term has its roots in marijuana culture, in which it describes equally odiferous and oily weed. Interestingly, the comparison actually has good scientific legs, as the hop plant, while pretty unique, is most closely related to hemp and nettles, and shares some of the same chemical properties. Contrary to popular mythology, however, hops do not contain THC, the main psychoactive compound in marijuana. Sorry.

SEE ALSO
Off flavours *p161*
Pediococcus p166

DIACETYL | FAULT

A distinctive buttery-aroma chemical, reminiscent of cinema popcorn and butterscotch. It's generally a sign of stressed or unhealthy yeast (which produces the main precursor chemical), though can also be a product of bacterial infection, particularly in dirty draft lines. At very low concentrations it can be acceptable in some English-style ales, but is otherwise considered an off aroma.

DISPENSING CASK | DRINKING

Unlike draft systems, which use gas to push beer up the line and into the glass under force, a cask-ale pump (or "beer engine", as it's sometimes rather grandly called) is a simple mechanism that sucks the liquid up when the server pulls down on a long mechanical handle. To prevent a vacuum building up inside the cask, it's common for the bung on top of the vessel to be left off when the pub is open and replaced at closing time. In some northern areas of the UK, an electric pump is used to draw beer up from the cask. This is a regional variation, and local beers are brewed to take account of the agitation and aeration caused by pumping. Some pubs even serve cask ale with the assistance of gas pressure. CAMRA takes a very dim view of such shenanigans.

DMS | FAULT

A common off aroma, redolent of tinned sweetcorn or old vegetables, dimethyl sulfide is formed during the boil, from a precursor found in grain – some grains more than others – and is usually boiled off by the end. In most styles and geographies it's a clear-cut fault (commonly indicative of a brewhouse problem), though in some light lagers, particularly in corn-heavy US macro-brewed affairs, it's actually part of the character that fans have come to expect. If the aroma is very noticeable, however, it may suggest an unwanted infection.

DOUBLE IPA | STYLE

See "American IPA" (page 20).

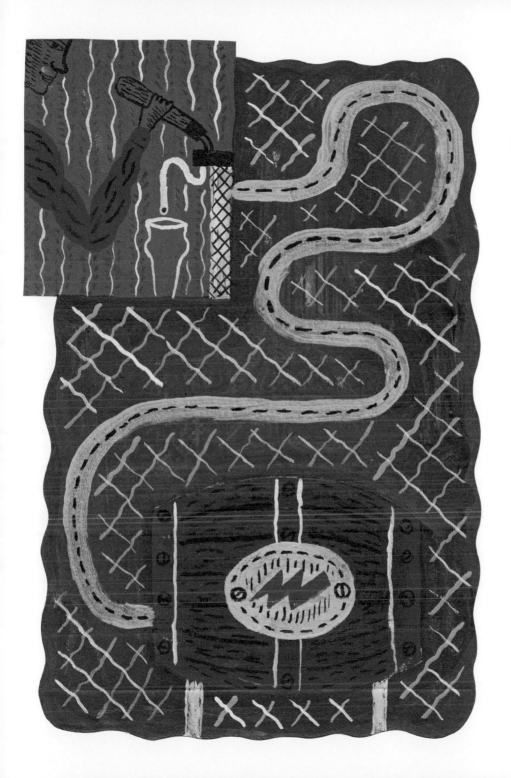

DRAFT SYSTEMS | BREWING

The complex arrangement of gases, liquids, pipes, valves and taps by which beer is transported from a pressurized keg into a beer glass at exactly the right temperature and consistency. In a field dominated by biology and chemistry, the correct setting up and maintenance of a draft system strays awfully close to maths, and should therefore be mistrusted by all right-thinking beer folk. In a nutshell, a draft system relies on the complex relationship between pressure and temperature in liquids and gases, in order to force beer out of a keg, up along a carefully measured length of tubing and out of the tap with enough force to create a pleasing head, but not so much force that it becomes a gassy, frothing mess.

DRUNKENNESS | DRINKING

Craft beer is about appreciation of taste, aroma and the brewer's skill. But it is also about getting drunk; drinking, when undertaken responsibly, makes us feel good. But why? When you start drinking, your liver kicks into action, metabolizing the ethanol into less harmful chemicals, including energy for the muscles and brain. This process takes time, though, and the liver can only do so much, so if there is more ethanol in your bloodstream than your liver can cope with, some of it goes on to mess with your physiology. It relaxes the muscles, dilates the capillary blood vessels and, perhaps most importantly, alters your brain chemistry in three main ways. It increases the effects of the neurotransmitter GABA, which keeps us calm, causing slurred speech, lack of coordination and sleepiness. Unencumbered by your usual worries, your inhibitions go out of the window, too. Ethanol also suppresses the natural stimulant glutamate, with an impact on coordination and speech. If you find there are sections of the evening you can't remember, that's glutamate suppression, too. Combine that with impaired judgment and an increased pleasure-seeking drive, and you have a recipe for both fun and regret. The third way alcohol messes with your brain is, sadly, addiction. Our brains respond to anything that stimulates our neurological "reward centre", calling us back time and time again for another hit. Alcohol, like most drugs, is great at ringing that bell; significantly better, in fact, than more legitimate stimuli such as food and water.

DRY-HOPPING | BREWING

The addition of hops after the wort has been cooled, either to the primary fermentation vessel, during secondary fermentation or even to the keg or cask. This approach means the alpha acids in the hops are never isomerized, limiting their bitterness but preserving their volatile flavour and aroma oils. For this reason, dry-hopping is often used in conjunction with bittering hops, added during the boil. The practice of dry-hopping isn't modern, as many assume; it originated centuries ago, when British brewers would add a handful of hops to the cask shortly before shipping it to the customer. While dry-hopping can take place any time after the wort has been cooled, it is generally agreed that during secondary fermentation is best. The amount of time the hops should be left in contact with the beer varies – a few days is usually sufficient, but if they are added to the keg or can they can be

SEE ALSO
Essential oils *p81*
Fermentation *p85*
Hop bursting *p117*
Hop torpedo *p118*
Hops, aroma *p120*
Secondary fermentation
 p198

in situ for weeks. This prolonged contact can give beer an oily or grassy character, which divides opinion.

DUBBEL | STYLE

A dark, complex-malted, relatively strong Belgian abbey ale that's been brewed by monks for hundreds of years. The use of colour malts is central to this style, bringing layers of malt character with hints of chocolate and rich, dried soft fruits. Hops are pretty mild and their main contribution is a certain spiciness, accentuated by a super-dry body and equally spicy/fruity yeast character. While it will always be most closely associated with Trappist breweries, several foreign craft breweries – particularly Belgium-obsessives like Allagash in the US – have made their own excellent *dubbels*.

DUNKEL | STYLE

According to the histories, *dunkel* was the original lager style, emerging from southern Germany in the 16th century. Ruby red, it would at first have been brewed entirely with amber Munich malt, though today you will often find a base of pilsner malt, with a dash of black malt to bring the colour down. *Dunkel* is all about the malt – hops don't get much of a look-in – with rich, sweet, dark, biscuity layers on the nose, and toffee with some soft, toasted notes on the palate.

SEE ALSO
Trappist *p223*
Tripel *p224*

ENZYMES | SCIENCE

Complex biological catalysts – essentially microscopic powerhouses for speeding up chemical reactions. In the brewing process, the enzymes found naturally on the husks of malted grain activate during mashing, at around 64°C (147°F), and work furiously to convert the starches and other long-chain carbohydrates around the kernel into sweet, fermentable sugar. There are a number of enzyme groups in the mash, each with its own important function. The amylases (alpha and beta) tend to get most of the limelight, as they're responsible for converting starch to fermentable maltose, but they definitely aren't the only show in town. Other groups do a similar job, snipping apart long proteins (which would otherwise cause haze and other problems) into smaller chunks that are useful for yeast nutrition, body and head retention.

ESSENTIAL OILS | INGREDIENT

Depending on the variety, most hops contain somewhere in the region of 250 essential oils, around 25 of which are known to contribute flavour and aroma to beer. The main three are myrcene, humulene and caryolene. Essential oils are highly volatile, meaning they evaporate easily. In fact, when you raise a glass of beer to your nose and inhale those wonderful hoppy aromas, you are actually smelling the volatile essential oils breaking down and evaporating from the beer's surface. This is also why aroma hops are added toward the end of the boil, in the whirlpool or even to the cooled wort: the more heat they are exposed to, the more essential oils are lost.

ESTERS | SCIENCE

Compounds formed during fermentation, from a reaction between organic acids in the wort and the developing alcohol. A real double-edged sword, at low levels esters can provide lip-smacking fruit character – pear, banana, apple, apricot and more – but beyond a certain concentration this becomes a distinctly unpleasant, solvent character reminiscent of nail-polish remover. Esters are most often found in high-alcohol beers and usually arise from yeast stress as a result of a too-high fermentation temperature or a lack of oxygen in the wort. Some yeasts have been bred to produce specific ester characters and are a key feature of many Belgian styles in particular.

FAKE CRAFT | BEER CULTURE

Craft now makes up 12 percent of the total US beer market, and some other countries aren't far behind. This may seem a relatively modest slice, but it represents a lot of cash and is growing all the time. It was perhaps inevitable that "Big Beer" would eventually sit up, take notice and try to cash in with their own offering on what is effectively a new, potentially lucrative market for "premium" beers. Whether their efforts, some of which are doing rather well commercially, deserve to be ranked alongside "genuine" craft products is a matter of fierce debate, particularly when Big Beer's chosen route into the market involves swallowing a beloved craft brand whole.

FERMENTATION | BREWING

In brewing terms, fermentation is something of a blanket term for the complex chemical reactions that take place between yeast (and sometimes bacteria) and the wort, the end result of which is delicious beer. Put very simply, fermentation is a reaction involving just three compounds: a sugar molecule, ethanol and carbon dioxide. The action of yeast "cuts up" the sugar molecule into the two waste products. But yeast moves in mysterious ways, and in reality this conversion involves no fewer than 11 different intermediate chemicals before we arrive at booze. Not only do we have 11 steps between sugar, ethanol and carbon dioxide, we have nearly 20 enzymes and co-enzymes (molecules that work with enzymes, such as vitamins) to assist with the reactions. These get to work in the fermentation reaction chain, cutting bonds between molecules to help make new molecules, changing the amount of phosphate, oxygen and hydrogen present, moving step by step closer to the end products.

Of course, fermentation is not as simple as sugar in, ethanol and carbon dioxide out. As well as ethanol, yeast can also create the shorter methanol molecule and much longer, oily fusel alcohols. Once in the wort, this cocktail of alcohols can set off further reactions, producing even more compounds. Ethanol, for example, becomes the sour-tasting carboxylic ethanoic acid, in a reaction known as "redox". Fragrant aldehydes can arise from the same reaction, as the midway stage between the alcohol and acid. Fruity esters are created when a carboxylic acid combines with an alcohol in a process called esterification. The ingredients of the wort have a major impact on the reactions that go on – beyond their obvious contribution of fermentable sugar – because of the effect they have on potential reactants. For example, oats are chock-full of natural nutrients and biologically active substances such as folate, magnesium, vitamins and antioxidants.

FERMENTATION TEMPERATURE | BREWING

No other environmental factor has as much influence on fermentation as temperature, as it determines a great deal about how the yeast will behave. Getting this even slightly

SEE ALSO
Spontaneous fermentation
  p208
Trub*p226*
Wort*p240*
Yeast*p243*

wrong can ruin a beer, or at least see it turn out quite differently from how you intended. In addition to alcohol and carbon dioxide, yeast produces hundreds of trace by-products during fermentation, which can contribute flavour, aroma and mouthfeel. Each strain of yeast will come with advice about its optimum brewing temperature range, and often warnings about the kind of by-products it will produce at higher and lower temperatures. In general terms, at a lower fermentation temperature ale yeast will struggle to "clean up after itself", leaving behind potentially unacceptable quantities of diacetyl (a buttery flavour) and acetaldehyde (a cider-like taste) in the finished beer. Higher fermentation temperatures cause yeast to produce more of the fruity esters and higher, solvent-like alcohols, giving rise to different flavour characteristics that may or may not be desirable. Lager-makers will use *Saccharomyces pastorianus* at much lower temperatures, around 5–10°C (41–50°F), where *S. cerevisiae* becomes dormant. Bavarians have been brewing lager for centuries, storing beers in cold alpine caves, where only the wild yeasts most tolerant to the cold would have survived; this heritage informs their choice of cold-fermenting lager yeasts to the present day.

FERMENTATION VESSEL | EQUIPMENT

Often referred to simply as a "fermenter" or even just an "FV" if you're really cool. At its most basic, this is the container that the wort sits in while the yeast is going to town on all those lovely sugars. Historically, fermentation vessels have taken many shapes and been made from many different materials, probably starting out with animal-skin sacks before progressing to earthenware, wooden barrels and eventually metal. Many traditional fermentation vessels would have been open to the air and therefore to any wild yeast and bacteria that might be hanging around. Generally speaking, unless you're using something like a foeder and want the beer to come into contact with resident microflora, your main requirements of a fermenter are that it is easy to clean, won't taint the beer and will protect fermentation from unwanted airborne microorganisms. The vast majority of modern breweries, therefore, use the familiar cylindroconical fermenter: a tall cylindrical stainless-steel tank with an inverted cone and spigot at the base. Patented by Leopold Nathan in 1927, this has many advantages over its forebears, primarily the ease of retrieving yeast from the cone.

FESTIVALS | BEER CULTURE

SEE ALSO
Drunkenness *p77*
Oktoberfest *p162*

If there's one area in which craft beer has without a shadow of a doubt improved things, it's beer festivals. Particularly in the UK, these used to be universally grim affairs, with rows of tables staffed by volunteers who, by and large, knew very little about what they were pouring. To anyone outside the mostly male crowd of knowledgeable beer lovers, they were at best baffling and at worst slightly intimidating. Today's festivals are altogether more rewarding and sociable affairs. It's quite normal to find the brewers, or at the very least brewery staff of some description, manning their stand and actively encouraging conversation. There's usually great food on hand, often live music and a good mix of ages, genders and backgrounds in attendance, all sharing their love of beer in an atmosphere of general bonhomie.

FESTIVALS – SURVIVAL | BEER CULTURE

There is such a thing as too much fun, though, and getting the most out of your beer festival involves a little discipline. Here are a few tips:

- Do your homework. Most festivals publish a list of breweries in attendance ahead of time. Some even produce beer lists. Figure out your "must-haves".
- Don't cry over bad beer. We all make mistakes – if you pick a duff beer, don't waste stomach space, just ditch it and move on.
- Stay hydrated. Some festivals (absurdly) don't supply free drinking water, so it's a good idea to take your own just in case.
- Keep your ear to the ground. Every festival has its "have you tried…?" beers, and there's nothing worse than only hearing about them after they're gone. Listen out for recommendations and keep an eye on social media to find out what's hot.

FESTIVE ALE | STYLE

Not an actual style in its own right, festive (or Christmas) ale is defined mostly by its marketing, but also (hopefully) by the sense of occasion it brings to the table. Generally big on flavour and at least generous in ABV, festive ales are rarely spiced – unlike their creepy cousin, pumpkin ale – preferring barrel-ageing, exotic malts and flamboyant presentation.

FILTRATION | BREWING

Given time and a competent brewer, most beers will become bright and clear on their own, as proteins and solids drop out under their own weight. To help this process along, fining is sometimes used to "pull" any unwanted gunk out of suspension. Filtration is an order of magnitude more invasive, and requires a delicate balance between aesthetics, stability and character.

In theory, modern filtration techniques can be so effective that even the tiniest particulates and bacteria are removed. Go too far, though, and you'll lose a lot of the good stuff too, including the proteins necessary for body and head formation, hop compounds and even colour. Whatever the current trend, it's always important to remember that filtering isn't automatically a good thing or a bad thing, and that a bright beer hasn't necessarily been filtered.

FINING | BREWING

SEE ALSO
Filtration *p91*
Haze *p110*

Given time and the right conditions, the haze that can form in beer during brewing and fermentation will often clear. Sometimes, though, if the style dictates that the finished beer should be extra bright, some form of "fining" is used. Traditionally, isinglass – made from the dried swim bladders of certain fish – has been the most common fining agent and is still widely used today, though gelatin and some synthetic agents do the same job of pulling yeast and other particles to the bottom of the tank for disposal.

FIRKIN | EQUIPMENT

SEE ALSO
Cask *p65*

A 40.9-litre (9-gallon) metal cask, a firkin is the standard vessel for real ales and has replaced the less reliable, less sanitary wooden version.

FLANDERS RED/BROWN | STYLE

These are Belgian beers brewed in the normal way, but then aged in open oak vats for up to two years, where they are infected by *Lactobacillus*, *Acetobacter* and *Brettanomyces* from the wood itself. This heady combination gives the beers a distinctive, complex sourness: tart and vinegary, with a funky, earthy quality which is balanced by the caramel and burnt sugar character of the malt. Both red and brown Flanders ales rely on skilled blending, often of old and new beers, to achieve the sweet/sour balance that characterizes this style. Sours are often used as a base for fruit beers, and cherry and raspberry Flanders beers are quite common. As a tricky style to get right, requiring skill and patience, Flanders red in particular has found some popularity among American craft brewers looking to prove their skills.

FLIGHT | DRINKING

A curated selection of beer samples, usually one third of a pint (190ml) each. The term originated in the wine world and was first used in this way during the late 1970s. It most likely comes from the collective noun meaning "a group of similar objects flying through the air together". If this feels overly poetic for beer, consider the alternative: asking for a flock, herd or gaggle of brews.

FLOCCULATION | SCIENCE

When they have finished the hard work of fermentation, yeast cells in suspension will naturally clump together in large blobs and drop to the bottom of the fermentation vessel, leaving the beer bright and clear. This is known (wonderfully) as flocculation, and is unique to brewer's yeast; as brewers have over the centuries collected yeast either from the top or bottom of the fermenter (depending on whether they are using top- or bottom-fermenting yeast), they have inadvertently selected ever more flocculant strains, and natural selection has taken its course. If yeasts flocculate too early, the resulting beer will be under-attenuated and sweet; too late and it will be cloudy with a yeasty taste. High-flocculating yeasts aren't automatically more desirable, though, and a brewer's choice of yeast will depend on the style being brewed. An English ale, for example, will usually employ a yeast with high flocculation, whereas something like a *hefeweizen* typically has low flocculation.

FOEDER | EQUIPMENT

SEE ALSO
Fermentation *p85*
Sour *p207*
Spontaneous fermentation
  p208
Yeast, wild *p245*

An increasingly common sight among adventurous US craft brewers, foeders (or foedres or foudres, depending on where you are) are traditional oak vessels, usually French oak, used primarily for long-term fermentation. They can range in size from small barrels right up to towering commercial-scale tanks. Slow fermentation typically involves wild yeast and bacteria in one form or another; these can take months to do their work, so foeders are most commonly associated with sour beer. Because of the long timescales involved, as well as the somewhat unpredictable nature of wood and wild cultures, foeder fermentation is considered a powerful demonstration of the brewer's craft.

GERMANY | ORIGIN

Beer is so engrained in German culture that it is hard (at least for the beer lover) to even think of the birthplace of Einstein, Beethoven and Charlemagne without a frothing amber *maß* of lager making its way into the picture. Germany is arguably the most prescriptive of the world's major beer cultures, thanks to the centuries-old *Reinheitsgebot* or "purity law", which lays down strict limits on what a "beer" can include, and to the general reverence for the country's lager-centric brewing traditions. And it is undoubtedly lager – clean, crisp and subtly hopped – for which Germany is best known and most respected. Yet within this seemingly narrow scope, there still exists a surprisingly broad array of styles, with fascinating regional variations (German culture is far from homogenized) and even some characterful exceptions to the *Reinheitsgebot*. With its deep historical roots and unflinching focus on quality, Germany is an inspiration for brewers the world over.

GLASSWARE | EQUIPMENT

The idea of having vessels specifically for beer goes back a very long way, and their design has always gone far beyond the purely functional. Like animals in the wild, they have been subject to evolution, with generations of change leading to the best designs for individual styles, delivering the perfect flavour, aroma and even emotional connection. Beer vessels are often a very personal thing and, to this day, it's not uncommon (particularly in Britain) for regulars at a pub to uphold the tradition of keeping their own mug behind the bar for their sole use. Beer-drinking vessels weren't typically made from glass until the late 19th century, when the industrialization of glassware caused prices to drop dramatically. Prior to this, beer would have been drunk out of earthenware, ceramic or metal jugs. Different designs are associated with different nationalities and styles of beer, and are often intended to enhance the unique characteristics of their contents. For example, tall, fluted glasses show off the colour and head of lagers, a style for which showcasing the aroma is less important. For Belgian ales, though, a round-bowled, stemmed glass with a slightly narrower top allows the contents to be swirled and traps the complex aromas for any waiting nose.

SEE ALSO
Reinheitsgebot p187

GOSE | STYLE

....

Gose is special among German beers for several reasons. First, it's an ale (it uses top-fermenting yeast) as opposed to a lager. Second, and most interestingly, it takes the country's sacred *Reinheitsgebot*, throws it on the floor and does a merry little Saxon dance on it. With 50 percent wheat, *Lactobacillus* sourness and the frequent addition of salt and spices, *gose* is more like a *Berliner weisse* than the lagers and pilsners we typically associate with Germany. It gets away with this behaviour by virtue of being a regional speciality. German beer politics aside, *gose* is a

very quenching, moreish style, great on a warm day, friendly to fruit, and finding favour among craft brewers in search of something a little different.

GRAVITY | TASTING

Gravity describes the density of the wort or beer, which in turn tells us how much sugar is present. By taking a reading of the original gravity (before the yeast is pitched) and the final gravity (once fermentation is complete), brewers can employ a simple formula to calculate how much of the sugar has been converted to ethanol, and therefore the ABV of the beer. Gravity is measured using a simple device called a hydrometer, or a more accurate electronic instrument called a refractometer. Broadly speaking, the process uses one of two scales: Degrees Plato, which simply gives the percentage of the liquid that is dissolved solids, and Original Gravity (OG), which is the ratio of the weight of the wort against the weight of the same volume of pure water. Belgium has its own scale, Belgian degrees, which works in much the same way as OG. Brewing recipes will include targets for original and final gravity, based on the quantity and type of malt being used, the efficiency of the equipment and the attenuation of the chosen yeast strain.

GREEN BEER | STYLE

A fine tradition of the hop harvest, made with green or "wet" hops, straight off the bine. This is trickier than it sounds, as hops once cut begin to compost in a matter of hours, giving green beer brewing a very narrow window and extremely limited volumes. The finished beer is best drunk

G

103

fresh, and is definitely worth seeking out; the green hops impart a uniquely light, grassy and zingy character, less pungent than regular dried-hop beer, but subtle and refreshing. Green beers are brewed wherever there is a hop harvest, and prolific growing regions often have their own festivals around harvest time.

GRIST | BREWING

Before the starches in malted cereal can be broken down into sugar during mashing in, the grains must be milled – broken up by crushing or rolling – into a coarse powder called grist. The grade of milling is extremely important: too coarse and parts of the seed will remain inaccessible, significantly reducing the efficiency of the brew; too fine and it will form a thick, impermeable porridge in the mash, again reducing efficiency and potentially bringing the entire process to a halt. Once milled, grain has a limited shelf life. When buying grain for brewing, therefore, it is a good idea to find a shop that will grind at the point of sale. Otherwise you have no idea how long the grist has been sitting there.

GROWLER | EQUIPMENT

Today's growlers are typically reusable, swing-top bottles that can be taken into taprooms and bottleshops to be filled directly from the cask or keg so that the contents can be consumed at home for maximum freshness (there are stainless-steel variants, too). Many such shops will even have a dedicated "growler station", which replicates the technology used on the bottling lines of commercial breweries to fill without oxygen, foam or contamination. The

use of growlers dates back to the late 17th century, when fresh beer – often consumed instead of drinking water, because it was sterile – would be carried home in a lidded galvanized bucket. One theory is that the name derives from the noise made when carbon dioxide escaped through the lid, as the beer sloshed around inside. Growlers have continued to be used on a small scale ever since, particularly in the UK, where the tradition of cask and real ale makes the ability to take fresh beer home particularly appealing. The preferred vessel has evolved from the buckets of yore, though, from waxed cardboard in the 1950s and '60s, to plastic PET bottles in the '80s and '90s, and onto metal vessels or swing-top bottles today.

GUEUZE | STYLE

SEE ALSO
Lambic *p141*
Sour *p207*

An artful, bottled blend of old and young lambics that gives a wonderfully complex character. *Gueuzes* can range from light, yogurt acidity to full-on vinegar sourness, often with tropical fruit notes and a strong oak influence. They are bottle-conditioned and are typically more heavily carbonated than ordinary lambics. Excellent examples of the style include Cantillon Gueuze 100% Lambic and Drie Fonteinen Oude Geuze, whose vintage series has become a mainstay among lambic fans.

HANGOVER | DRINKING

The aftermath of chemical havoc wreaked on your body and mind following the ingestion of a potent neurotoxin: booze. While the exact physiological mechanisms behind the hangover remain something of a mystery, we know some of what happens and why. First, there's the obvious dehydration, and it's definitely true that drinking a pint of water before slumping into bed will help somewhat. As it's metabolizing ethanol, your liver also produces acetaldehyde, another kind of toxin that needs to be broken down in its turn. In addition, alcohol is a powerful depressant, which will leave you feeling generally sorry for yourself in any case, exacerbating any other ill effects. There are many supposed "cures", including the consumption of raw eggs. Many people swear by a "hair of the dog", but there's little evidence this does any good beyond the mild analgesic effect of the alcohol itself. It should be noted that a hangover is quite different from alcohol poisoning, a much more serious condition in which a toxic amount of ethanol is consumed in a short period. Symptoms can include vomiting, hypothermia, unconsciousness and fitting. This can't be slept off or caffeinated away – medical help should be sought immediately.

HAZE | FAULT

Our obsession with super-clear beer isn't by any means a new phenomenon, and a plethora of techniques for ensuring pin-sharp liquid – from filtration to fining – has been added to the brewer's arsenal over the centuries. However, there is still a lot that can go wrong, resulting in hazy beer and, invariably, complaints from unhappy customers. Chill haze is most common in unfiltered beers, including a lot of craft ales. When the beer is chilled, proteins already present in the liquid group together and fall out of solution, creating a harmless, flavourless haze that dissipates again once the temperature rises. If a bottle-conditioned beer is poured ineptly, or hasn't had opportunity to settle properly, yeast sediment can be disturbed and swirl through the beer. This affects the taste and, unless it's a deliberate part of the style, is definitely to be avoided. Microbiological infection can also cause haze. If you're served an unexpectedly hazy pint, which also has a sour or vinegary edge, send it back. Finally, if a beer is well past its sell-by date or has been mis-stored, you may well observe a "snow globe" effect in the bottle. This is the result of complex protein structures breaking down and precipitating out of the liquid. Some styles, of course, such as *hefeweizen* and *witbier*, are deliberately hazy (indeed, *hefeweizen* is traditionally served from the bottle in a way that *enhances* its haziness), but as usual modern craft brewers are pushing the boundaries of what has traditionally been acceptable. For example, the craze for North East IPAs (NEIPAs) resulted in some positively soupy concoctions, and rumours abound of some unscrupulous brewers adding flour to their beer to enhance its cloudiness.

HEAD | TASTING

Whether it's a brilliant, creamy white meringue or a sticky, lacy topping, the head of a beer is a vital component in flavour, aroma, aesthetics and generally the whole beer-drinking experience. People get very worked up about it. The head is made up of bubbles of beer-enclosed gas, which precipitate from the liquid as it is poured and rise to the surface. Molecules called surfactants in the beer gather around the bubble's wall, limiting the amount of gas that can get inside and keeping it small. These same surfactants also contribute to the bubble's stability when it reaches the surface, allowing the head to stay solid rather than just fizzing away. Surfactants are special to beer, as they result from a combination of the molecules present in grain (particularly malt and wheat) and hops. One without the other would not produce the same result. One of the most important factors in head formation and beer bubbles generally is the presence of a "site of nucleation". This is a slightly over dramatic way of saying "a rough surface on which the bubbles can form". Most beer glasses are specially created to have a microscopic texture on their inner base, giving carbon dioxide dissolved in the beer somewhere to coalesce, leading to the formation of those all-important, head-creating bubbles.

HOME-BREW | BREWING

For some beer lovers, the thrill of a perfect pint comes not only from the drinking, but from the creation itself. Of course, the idea of home-brewing predates the advent of the commercial brewery by thousands of years, and many successful professional brewers started out with 30-litre (6½-gallon) kettles in their (or their parents') garage, learning from their mistakes on a small scale. In many countries, the 20th century saw home-brewing circumscribed by tax or law, though by the late 1970s most restrictions had been removed. At this time, home-brewing was seen largely as a way of making cheap beer, often to a standard equal to, or even better than, the poor selection of beers available on the supermarket shelf. For a time, the majority of home-brewers used simple kits containing yeast, liquid malt extract and hop extract, which were added to water and left to ferment for a couple of weeks. In recent years, however – partly thanks to the growing popularity of craft beer – there has been a significant rise in specialist home-brew stores and in "all-grain" home-brewing, which uses whole ingredients rather than extracts, for better results. Technology has also improved, with the availability of high-quality home-brew systems – including the Grainfather, Braumeister and others – bringing home-brewers closer to a scaled-down commercial-grade setup.

HOME-BREW EQUIPMENT | EQUIPMENT

Even all-grain home-brewing can be achieved with pretty modest equipment, much of which can be found in any ordinary kitchen. There are a few bits of kit you should definitely have to hand before starting out, though:

- A large stock pot for mashing and boiling, or better yet two
- A broad, sturdy sieve, capable of holding a large quantity of malt
- A kettle

- A large jug
- A long-handled spoon
- A thermometer
- Sanitizing solution
- Citric acid, for cleaning
- Some means of cooling wort, usually a counter-flow chiller, an immersion chiller or even a large tub of iced water
- A siphon for transferring wort
- A glass carboy or plastic fermentation bucket, with an airlock
- Bottling kit.

HOP BURSTING | BREWING

A popular technique for extracting maximum aroma from hops without a whole lot of accompanying bitterness. Rather than adding all the hops at the beginning of the boil, all or most are held back until the final few minutes, or even added to the whirlpool. The volatile essential oils, which impart those wonderful aromatic qualities, are not boiled away, while the hops' alpha acids are not exposed to prolonged heat, limiting isomerization and therefore bitterness.

HOP PELLETS | INGREDIENT

An alternative to whole-cone hops, frequently used in home-brew, though also sometimes in commercial production. Once dried, hops destined for pelleting are hammer-milled, creating a tacky powder, then forced through an extrusion die in a process similar to that used to produce dried animal feed, and typically sold in vacuum-sealed foil bags to protect from both light and oxygen. The quality of the pellets depends very much on the temperature and speed of this extrusion process: too hot or too fast, and the delicate hops can suffer from scorching and oxidation, leading to noticeable off flavours in the finished beer. There are pros and cons to hop pellets. On the plus side, the fact that they dissolve during the boil, and that milling ruptures the lupulin glands, increases hop utilization by some 10 percent. Conversely, they do tend to make a sludgy mess in the kettle or fermenter, and sometimes require additional filtering. Some brewers also see them as less natural and claim the milling process impairs their flavour and aroma.

HOP TORPEDO | BREWING

Pioneered by California's Sierra Nevada brewery, hop torpedos are now a popular way for commercial-scale breweries to dry-hop their brews using whole-cone hops (previously, they would probably have used hop pellets or extract, which were more efficient and easier to handle). Despite looking like a moon lander, the principle behind the hop torpedo is very simple – it's a small tank containing a chamber of hop cones, through which beer is circulated from a larger tank over the course of a few days. The main advantages are that the messy whole hops never get into the main vessel, yet the constant circulation and loose distribution of the hops within the torpedo chamber ensure maximum efficiency.

HOP TRENDS | BEER CULTURE

If the craft revolution of recent years has changed one thing, it's how we perceive the humble hop plant. Since macro-scale lager brewers began to dominate in the 1970s, the prevailing orthodoxy has been that hops should not shout too loudly; their job was to provide a clean, one-dimensional bitterness to balance out the pilsner malts in supermarket lagers whose one goal was "drinkability". Hop breeders despaired of this situation and, until very recently, the idea of breeding a hop variety for its aroma or unusual flavour profile was simply absurd. This started to turn around in the US in the 1980s and '90s, when tiny West Coast pioneers such as Anchor and Sierra Nevada looked to the brash, fruity hop varieties that thrived in their part of the world, which gave beers not only bitterness but juicy aromas and flavours quite unlike anything else that existed at the time. The sudden popularity of "hop-forward" IPAs and APAs changed everything. Previously obscure US varietals, not to mention equally bombastic new hops from elsewhere in the world, such as New Zealand's Nelson Sauvin, have become household names, and thousands of craft breweries around the world are clamouring for exciting and exotic new options.

HOPS | INGREDIENT

The hop plant itself (*Humulus lupulus*) is a bona fide botanical oddity. The hop "cones" are part fruit, part flower and can be found growing on lush, spreading "bines" throughout the world's warm, wet, temperate regions. They've been used in brewing for hundreds of years. Hops are highly regional, and each growing region has its own distinctive varieties and styles. They are also extremely sensitive to soil, sunlight, air and weather conditions – the same hop grown in different countries will have subtle but real differences – leading some to argue they have as strong a claim to terroir as wine grapes. At the heart of the cone is a small stem, surrounded by gossamer petal-like leaves and – most importantly – tiny specks of a waxy, bright yellow substance called lupulin. This is the source of the hop's beer-making power, providing flavour, aroma and antiseptic properties. In addition to the resinous alpha and beta acids that are so crucial for imparting bitterness, it also contains hundreds of distinct aromatic oils, which vary according to variety and geography, and can include pine, mint, grass, resin, mango, citrus and a range of other herbal, spice, floral and fruit flavours and aromas.

HOPS, AROMA | INGREDIENT

SEE ALSO
Boil *p48*
Dry-hopping *p78*
Essential oils *p81*
Hop torpedo *p118*
Wort *p240*

As the name suggests, these are hops used to add aroma and non-bittering flavours to a beer. They are often lower in alpha acids (5 percent or less) but rich in aroma-imparting essential oils; they are added to the wort later in the boil, or even dry-hopped to maximize their effect. Many hops can be used both for bittering and aroma; Citra, for example, might be added at two stages, with a quantity at the beginning of the boil, so that its plentiful alpha acids isomerize for bitterness, and a second batch right at the end, to capture the hop's distinctive lemon and tropical fruit notes. A good deal of attention has been paid over the past few decades to new methods for getting the most out of aroma hops, leading to innovations such as dry-hopping, hop torpedos and even "hoppinators" – canisters of whole hops plumbed directly into the serving line for a final shot of essential oils as the beer passes through.

HOPS, BITTERING | INGREDIENT

SEE ALSO
Alpha acid *p17*
Boil *p48*

Typically high in alpha acids but low in volatile aromatic oils, bittering hops are added early in the boil, to maximize isomerization.

H

120

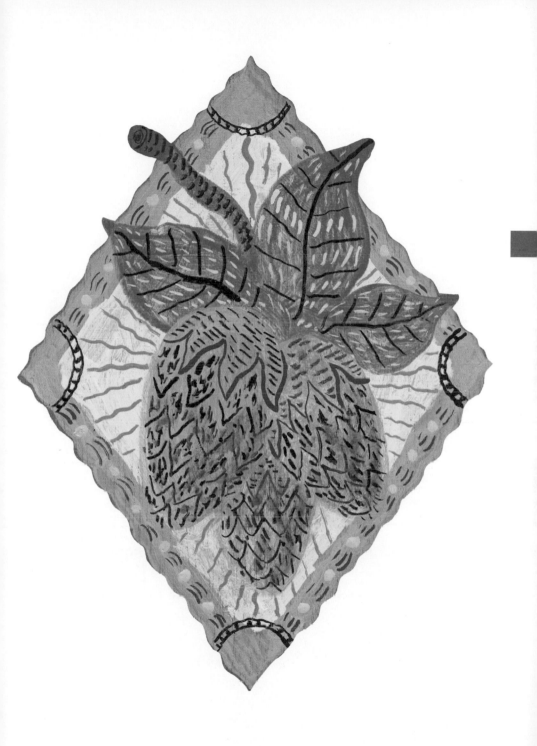

HOPS, BREEDING | SCIENCE

Many of the world's most popular hop varietals
have been grown with great consistency for
centuries. Yet there are also new hops constantly
being developed, bred for specific characteristics
including flavour, aroma, bitterness, yield
and greater resistance to weather, pests and
disease. The commercial appetite for new hops,
and for hops with novel flavour and aroma
characteristics, has rocketed thanks to the
growth of the international craft movement,
and plants that would previously have been
discarded as non-commercial oddities are
being actively selected. Development of a new
hop varietal – from the initial cross through to
commercialization – typically takes at least a
decade, and involves a great deal of breeding
and selection on the ground, as well as working
with breweries on how the hops will be used
in practice. Such development is undertaken
by a few specialist businesses, such as the Hop
Breeding Company in the US and Wye Hops
in the UK.

HOPS, HARVESTING | BREWING

Hop farms or gardens have a lot in common
with vineyards, both in appearance and in the
care that must be taken in maintaining the
delicate crop each year. Tall poles mark out the
broad lines of plants, between which are hung
thick strings for the hop bines to climb. When
the season is right, the bines grow incredibly
quickly, and shaping them for the optimum yield
(as well as dealing with any pests and diseases)
is a labour-intensive task. One of hops' many
idiosyncrasies is that they are very sensitive to
day length. Hop cones will only begin to form

when the days are precisely the right length, and the plant usually starts and ends its annual cycle on roughly the same day each year, whatever the weather happens to be doing. This makes them susceptible to frosty late springs, for example. When the harvest is ready (in the UK, it is traditionally completed before the autumn equinox) the bines are cut around 30cm (1ft) above the ground, and the long garlands of cones are loaded onto trucks for drying. This part of the process is critical as, once cut, the fragile cones begin to decay and compost within hours, and must be rushed to the oast house for drying. At the oast house, the cones are separated from the bines (which are then discarded) and piled into kiln driers – broad, shallow tanks with perforated bases, through which hot air is passed until the the hops are stable and dry. Once dried, the hops are either compressed and packed whole, or undergo additional processing to be turned into pellets. In either form, they are usually packed in foil or some other material that protects them from ultraviolet light.

HOT BREAK | BREWING

When mashing and sparging are complete, and the wort is just starting to boil, a thick foam will rise to the top, comprised mostly of protein from the grain. After around five minutes of boiling (or sometimes longer, if there is more protein), the foam will have dissipated and, thanks to the constant rolling of the boil, these proteins and other matter will have clumped together into easily visible particles; this is hot break. Once the boil is finished, these heavy clumps of matter will drop to the bottom of the kettle and can be discarded. This is a vital part of the brewing process, as without hot break the protein can remain in suspension, causing chill haze and other problems in the finished beer.

HYDROMETER | EQUIPMENT

A simple scientific instrument for measuring the amount of sugar and other dissolved solids in water (or "gravity"), consisting of a weighted glass float, attached to a long glass scale. The hydrometer is dropped into a solution (wort, in the case of brewing beer) and a reading is taken from the scale at the point where it breaks the surface. In pure water, it will sink quite a long way, but in a more dense solution – suggesting a higher level of sugar and dissolved solids – it will float higher, giving a higher reading on the scale. While a vital tool in the brewer's arsenal, the hydrometer isn't pinpoint accurate, and larger breweries often use more sophisticated electronic equipment to measure gravity accurately.

SEE ALSO
Siebel Institute, The *p203*

IBD | BEER CULTURE

Arguably the world's foremost professional body for those working in the brewing and distilling industries, the UK-based Institute of Brewing and Distilling works with other institutions to provide training and qualifications to the next generation of technically expert brewers. Other respected beer research and education institutions exist across the world, notably the American Siebel Institute.

SEE ALSO
ABV *p13*

IMPERIAL | STYLE

Historically, "Imperial" was the designation given to beers imported to Britain from the court of the Russian Empire, and was little more than a badge of quality. In today's craft scene it's more synonymous with strength (in terms of both ABV and flavour) than anything else, and is applied liberally to a range of styles, seemingly interchangeable with "double", which itself generally means double the ABV for any given style; for example a "double IPA" will typically be around 9 percent ABV.

SEE ALSO
ABV *p13*
Barrel-ageing *p34*
Stout *p212*

IMPERIAL STOUT | STYLE

The 18th-century Imperial family of Russia loved a bit of stout, though apparently at a much higher alcoholic strength than their weedy British and Irish peers. Imperial stouts typically come in at 8 percent-plus ABV, often much higher, with a robust flavour profile and rich, viscous mouthfeel to match. While Imperial stouts are now brewed across the world, they remain a hugely popular style among Russian brewers and throughout the Baltic States. They are often barrel-aged in order to mellow out some of the harsher boozy notes and to add layers of flavour.

SEE ALSO
American IPA *p20*
Pale ale *p165*

IPA | STYLE

Strictly speaking, English IPA (India Pale Ale) should probably just be a subcategory of pale ale and bitter, yet it is so significant in the rise of the craft beer movement that it deserves its own entry. Among the first pale ales brewed specifically for export to India was that produced by Bow Brewery in London, in the late 18th century. Being close to the East India Docks, the brewery was a firm favourite among East India Company traders, and this is probably why it was selected as the company's export brewer of choice. More heavily hopped than an ordinary pale ale and higher in alcoholic strength (both factors which prevented it from spoiling), this new IPA was found to fare much better on the long journey to India, and the time at sea was even thought to improve its character. Although the distinction between pale ales, bitters and IPAs became a little murky, as English beers and styles were exported globally, the idea of a hop-forward, high-strength style captured the imagination of American brewers in the late 20th century, leading to a huge global renaissance for the style.

I

IRISH MOSS | INGREDIENT

Irish moss (*Chrondus crispus*) is a common seaweed found in abundance on the Atlantic coast of Europe and North America. In brewing, it is used as a fining agent, as it is rich in carrageenan, a substance with a negative electrostatic charge. As protein masses that form in the wort's hot break are positively charged, they are attracted to the Irish moss, making it more likely they will drop out of suspension and never make it into the fermenter, resulting in clearer beer. Irish moss has no direct impact on flavour, and a little goes a long way. Because of its high carrageenan content, it is also prized as the source of a thickening agent and stabilizer in the food industry, for products such as ice cream.

JUDGING | BEER CULTURE

Being invited to judge a beer competition is
a great honour, and is generally taken very
seriously by those involved, who are typically
selected for their expertise and impartiality.
Judging usually follows a highly structured,
methodical process, with beers tasted "blind"
(that is, with no knowledge of the brewer or
other information that could introduce bias)
and scored against set criteria, which vary from
competition to competition. While it sounds
like great fun – and is, to be honest – judging
is also a lot of work. Larger competitions will
involve multiple rounds to narrow the entry
down to the winners, and you will be tasting
a lot of beers (and potentially a lot of styles) in
fairly quick succession. If you're interested
in getting involved, volunteering behind the
scenes at a competition is a great way to start,
and several certification programmes exist for
those wanting to become a fully fledged judge.

KEG | EQUIPMENT

The kegs you find in pubs, bars and restaurants are stainless-steel (or occasionally aluminium) pressure vessels, into which beer is pumped, along with carbon dioxide, at the brewery. They have a single opening at the head, which connects to a hollow internal "spear" reaching down to the bottom of the keg. Once tapped, gas from an external canister (usually a mix of carbon dioxide and nitrogen, to prevent the beer from over-carbonating over time) is pumped in from the top of the keg, forcing the beer downward into the spear, back up through the "coupler" at the top of the keg and along the line for serving. Properly refrigerated – and depending somewhat on the style – kegs will keep for several months once tapped. This is one of several advantages they have over casks in the eyes of brewers and bar owners. Being made from stainless steel, however, kegs are both heavy and expensive. Once they're empty, they are typically returned to the brewer (or to a third party, if the brewery has rented them) for cleaning and then refilling. Some breweries stencil their names onto the keg, while others prefer to mark them with colour-coded bands, but keg theft is still a problem in some places.

K
133

KEGGERATOR | EQUIPMENT

A refrigerator adapted to hold a keg (or kegs) with holes for the tubing up and out to a tap. As an alternative, "keezers" are similarly adapted freezers with a setback thermostat to hold the temperature at the correct level for beer.

KETTLE | EQUIPMENT

See "Boil kettle" (page 48).

KEYKEG | EQUIPMENT

A one-way disposable keg that allows small breweries in particular an easy, hygienic way of kegging their beers without needing to invest in cleaning equipment or the high capital cost of traditional stainless-steel kegs. A keykeg consists of a sterile plastic bag contained by a hard plastic pressure vessel. Unlike a traditional keg, where the serving gas is pumped into the same chamber as the beer, forcing it out and along the serving line, in a keykeg gas is pumped into the void between the bag and the rigid case. As the gas never comes into contact with the beer, any pressurized gas, including oxygen, can be used. Some much larger breweries now also use keykegs for export, as their one-way nature eliminates the expense and logistical headache of repatriating empty steel kegs. Unromantic as keykegs look, you can visit the yards of 180-year-old Belgian Trappist breweries and see stacks of them destined for export.

KILNING | BREWING

The process of heating the germinated grain to dry it, halt growth and develop a range of malty

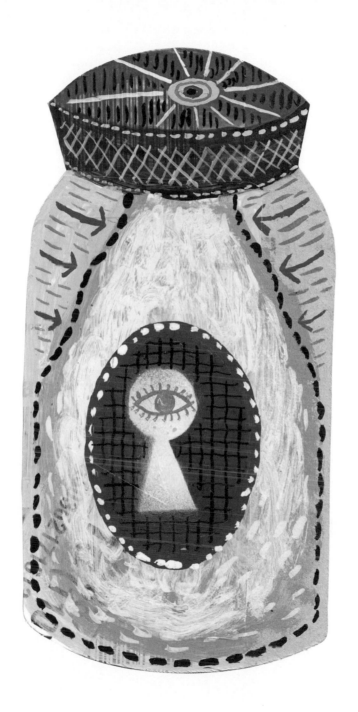

flavours. Most of the malt used in brewing is kilned gently at relatively low temperatures, to avoid destroying the all-important enzymes it contains. Kilning is typically carried out over several stages, depending on the desired character of the beer being brewed, and individual maltsters often have their own distinctive processes. Kilns are relatively simple vessels, with a heat source at the bottom, several tiered trays for grain, so that air can circulate between them, and a vent at the top.

LACTOBACILLUS | SCIENCE

A relatively fast-acting family of fermenting bacteria, which convert sugars into lactic acid and usually small amounts of acetic acid in the production of sour beers. There are many strains, each with slightly different characteristics in terms of their optimum fermentation conditions and flavour profile. *Lactobacillus* is the most common type of bacteria used in kettle sours, and typically imparts a light, clean tartness with notes of tangy yogurt. Some brewers introduce their *Lactobacillus* from wild sources, such as yogurt or unmashed grain. Most, however, go for commercially available liquid or freeze-dried products, which offer greater predictability and consistency.

LACTOSE | INGREDIENT

A complex sugar derived from milk, commonly used in dark beers, most notably in milk stouts. Since lactose is unfermentable, it stays around to give sweetness, viscosity and a creamy mouthfeel to the beer. It is available online and from home-brew shops as a fine white powder, and can be added to the brew in the kettle or the fermenter. In modern brewing, it is used instead of the whole milk that would traditionally have been added to some stouts and porters.

LAGER (DEFINITION 1) | STYLE

A popular, traditional family of beers arising from Bavaria and the surrounding areas, characterized by a crisp, clean malt profile, subdued use of noble hops and crystal-clear presentation. Lagers are brewed using bottom-fermenting yeast, almost exclusively of the strain *Saccharomyces pastorianus*, whose low fermentation and conditioning temperature ensures that very few flavour- and aroma-imparting by-products such as esters are produced to sully the beer's intended focus on malt and hops. Contrary to many people's expectations, lagers can run the full balance gamut, from stridently malty to lip-puckeringly hoppy. Hop selection is almost always from the classic German playbook, with noble hops painting from a refined palette of herbal, minty flavours, perhaps with just a dash of fruit if they're feeling whimsical. The name "lager" comes from the German word for storage or warehouse, and reflects the fact that lagers undergo a weeks-long secondary fermentation (or "lagering") at very low temperatures to ensure the yeast has the chance to mop up any residual waste products and the beer is perfectly smooth and clean. There should be little or no fermentation character present in the final beer. The lager family encompasses several distinct and surprisingly diverse styles, including pilsner, *helles*, *märzen*, *dunkel*, *bock* and *rauchbier*.

LAGER (DEFINITION 2) | STYLE

Tasteless, mass-produced muck aimed at people who don't really like beer, brewed by companies that care more about profit and

global domination than they do about quality. While this is clearly a gross generalization, it is absolutely fair to say that lager and the craft beer movement don't have the best relationship. Indeed, much as craft has sought to define itself by its commitment to independence, provenance, ingredients and the skill of the brewer, it is also undeniably a reaction against what its pioneers saw as the lager-based evils of "big brewing". There might be hope, though. What the craft movement really railed against in the 1980s and '90s was the phenomenon of US lagers, particularly "light" lagers, which had ceased to have much to do with their German and Czech antecedents. If you scratch the surface, you find a huge amount of respect for German brewing tradition; I have been told by many US brewers that, if it were up to them, they'd ditch their IPAs and brew only German styles under the *Reinheitsgebot*. The main challenge, it seems, is to persuade drinkers that they need to forgive and forget the damage that macro-brewed lagers have done to national beer traditions, and remind them that there is a whole world of crisp, clean, bottom-fermented loveliness to be explored.

LAMBIC | STYLE

One of the most singular and objectively wondrous beer styles in the world. Brewed in a specific region within and around Brussels (the name lambic is a protected appellation, like champagne or sherry), it is a truly ancient, wild-fermented style, marked by a sour, funky, fruity nose, acidic palate and seemingly endless levels of complexity. Even in purely mechanical brewing terms, lambic is weird stuff, with 60–80 percent of the mash bill consisting of unmalted wheat. This results in an extremely protein-rich wort that requires several hours' boiling to drive off unwanted compounds. The hops used should ideally be several years old so that they have lost most of their aroma and bitterness, as they're wanted primarily for their antimicrobial properties.

Fermentation, however, is really where this style's brewing science meets something more like religion. Lambic uses spontaneous fermentation, which was traditionally achieved by exposing the wort to the various airborne microorganisms that would drift in from the surrounding orchards. To this day, the true sources of the very specific balance of microbes responsible for lambic's unique character are something of a mystery. So much so that when Lindemans expanded its brewery just outside Brussels some years ago, it famously removed one wall from the old brewhouse and grafted it onto the side of the new one, so that whatever magic was in the structure itself would be transferred. After *E. coli* has dealt with the small amount of glucose in the wort, plain old *Saccharomyces* yeast comes in and does the heavy lifting of fermentation. Long, slow wood-ageing then allows *Brettanomyces*, *Pediococcus* and even sherry yeast to do their thing, souring and maturing the beer into ever more complex layers of flavour and aroma. While spontaneously fermented lambic-style sour beers are brewed elsewhere, lambic's reliance on local microfauna ensures it remains unique in the beer world. In relation to lambics as a whole, the fruit variety is a relatively modern innovation, but has become a popular and common sight in beer bars. It includes cherry (*kriek*), raspberry (*framboise*), peach, cassis and others.

LAUTER | BREWING

See "Sparge" (page 207).

LIGHT STRIKE | FAULT

SEE ALSO
Bottles *p51*
Macro-brewing *p145*
Off flavours *p161*

An off-flavour resulting from exposure to ultraviolet light, particularly sunlight. Iso-alpha acids from hops break down in such light and react with the sulfur naturally present in beer to form a compound known as MBT, a key component of the foul-smelling chemical deterrent that skunks spray. It is often said that a light-struck beer is "skunked"; it will have a dusty, vegetal taste, often with eggy notes. Brown bottles are effective at protecting beer from ultraviolet light, but not 100 percent; the only way to avoid it completely is to use cans. Clear and green glass offers no protection at all, and beer stored in such bottles can become light-struck very quickly. The only exceptions are those brewed with a treated hop extract called Tetrahop, which has the volatile chemical removed – these tend to be macro-brewed commercial lagers.

LIQUOR | BREWING

SEE ALSO
Water *p231*

The correct term for water used in brewing. Apprentices who absent-mindedly referred to it as "water" used to face their wages being docked.

MACRO-BREWING | BREWING

SEE ALSO
American lager *p20*
Fake craft *p85*
Selling out *p198*

Large-scale, industrial brewing. While macro-scale brewers arguably have their own craft, the term is often used to set "cheap", low-quality, mass-produced beers apart from more complex micro-brewed fare. It was the seemingly inevitable dominance of these global brewing behemoths – and the threat that precious national brewing cultures would be completely annihilated – that spurred the birth of the craft movement. This is why many craft beer lovers (and fans of traditional brewing) have such a visceral hatred of the big guys and everything they touch.

MAILLARD BROWNING | SCIENCE

SEE ALSO
Kilning *p134*
Malting *p146*

Describes the wide range of chemical changes that take place when you combine a carbohydrate or sugar with a nitrogenous substance (usually a protein) and heat it in the presence of moisture. Maillard browning explains why toast goes brown, and is the reason we can get so many different characters from the same malted grain depending on how we heat it. The actual chemical science is far beyond the scope of this book, but the important thing to remember is that kilning – which causes browning in malt – is a deceptively versatile and nuanced process, able to tease out flavour and aroma characteristics ranging from coffee and chocolate to dried fruit and toffee from a humble grain of malted barley.

MAIZE | INGREDIENT

See "Corn" (page 71).

MALT EXTRACT | INGREDIENT

An ingredient that will be familiar to anyone with home-brewing experience. While malt extract is generally seen as inferior to the all-grain alternative, it has the advantages of being easy to work with and giving very predictable results. In certain specific circumstances, several highly regarded international craft breweries use malt extract in some of their recipes. Malt extract production begins with brewing up a standard wort, which is then concentrated by heating it in a vacuum until it has reduced to a thick, sweet syrup. A side effect of this process is the production of the pigment melanoidin, which darkens the extract and also the resulting beer; so a beer made using malt extract will always be darker than the equivalent beer made with an all-grain process. It will also typically have a higher concentration of unfermentable dextrins (again, thanks to the concentration process), meaning it will start and finish fermenting at a higher gravity.

MALTING | BREWING

The process of partially germinating grains in order to unlock their starch reserves ready for them to be converted to sugar. During malting, grains are soaked or "steeped" for several days, until their water content rises

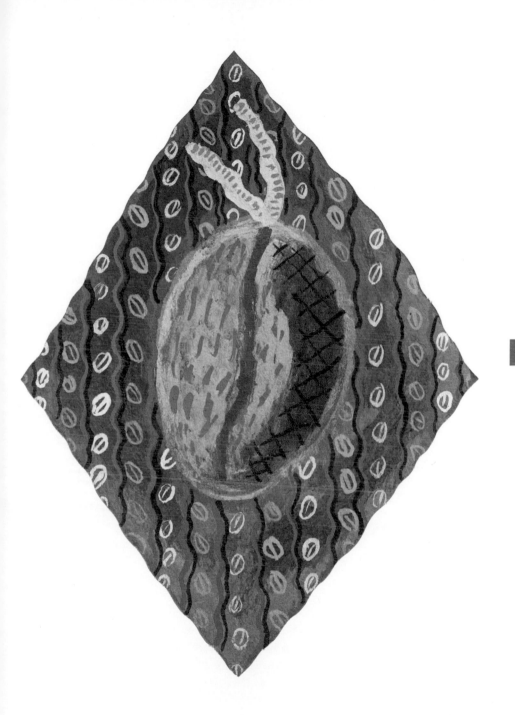

from about 12 percent to 40 percent or more. The absorbed water activates naturally occurring enzymes, which in turn break down the protein and carbohydrate barrier that protects the starch granules within. The grains are then transferred to a chamber where they are aerated with humid air (they need oxygen at this point) and where they are kept in gentle motion to prevent their growing rootlets weaving together into mats. If germination were allowed to continue, the all-important starch reserves would be consumed by the rapid growth of a sprout, and the grain would then be useless for fermentation. Instead, it is stopped in its tracks by kiln-drying for several hours; it is the temperature and duration of this kiln-drying that is the source of almost all malt flavour.

MALTS, BASE | INGREDIENT

Base malts are lightly kilned and serve as the bulk of the mash bill in any brew, even in very dark styles such as porters and stouts, as they provide a great flavour backbone and a high ratio of fermentable sugars. Individual styles include pilsner malt (the very lightest available), pale ale malt, Vienna malt (typically used in amber beers) and mild ale malt (a classic base for traditional dark English ales).

MALTS, COLOUR | INGREDIENT

Sometimes referred to as "kilned" malts, colour malts have a much greater colour range than base malts and usually make up only a small proportion of any recipe. Aromatic and dark Munich malts are used in brown beers, imparting a sweet caramel character to the final brew. Amber or biscuit malt has a very distinctive flavour of brown toast, while brown malt's smooth roasted notes make it perfect for porters.

MALTS, CRYSTAL AND CARAMEL | INGREDIENT

Made using quite a different process to the other malt types, these malts have a unique character. Rather than being dry-kilned, the wet malt is "stewed" at a relatively low temperature, causing the sugars within to caramelize. Bite down on a grain treated in this way and you will notice a distinct cracking crunch, and the flavour of caramel, burnt sugar and even dried fruit. These malts can range in colour from very pale to rich brown, depending on how long they have been heated. The very light dextrin malt is sometimes added to a recipe to aid body and head retention, while some darker crystal malts have a delicious chocolate aroma. There are many variables at play in the production of crystal and caramel malts, which can be tweaked to produce an exceptionally wide range of flavours and aromas.

MALTS, ROASTED | INGREDIENT

Typically used in small quantities to add colour and specific top notes to a recipe, usually chocolate and coffee bitterness. Colour-wise, roasted malts range from dark brown to intense black. As you move up this scale, though, the flavour and aroma become oddly less intense, as many flavour-imparting chemicals are destroyed or removed as the temperature and duration of the roast increase. For example, chocolate malt has a sharp, noticeably roasted character, whereas black malt has a much softer chocolate taste, and is often found in stouts and porters.

SEE ALSO
Porter p173
Stout p212

MASH | BREWING

The dense, porridgy soup of crushed grains and warm liquor that is the starting point of any brew. Mashing isn't just about hydrating the grain; even at this stage, there is real chemistry at work, and a mistake can ruin the whole enterprise. Malted barley contains a number of enzymes which, given the right conditions, will set to work breaking grain starches (long-chain carbohydrates) down into fermentable sugars and unfermentable dextrins (shorter carbohydrates). Each enzyme group performs a slightly different task and prefers a slightly different temperature to do its work. So, a relatively cool mash at 63°C (145°F) will produce a very fermentable wort and, depending on the yeast used, a dry final beer, while a warmer mash will produce more large, unfermentable sugars, which will remain in the final beer, making it noticeably sweeter. Brewers can adjust the temperature of their mash part way through the process to achieve different effects. Mashing typically takes around an hour and is followed by sparging or lautering.

MASH TUN | EQUIPMENT

The brewhouse vessel in which the ground malt (grist) is mixed with water at a controlled temperature, creating a thick porridge (mash) in which the grain starches are converted to sugars. Most mash tuns are temperature-controlled, with insulated walls to maintain the optimum temperature for the enzymes to do their work. In home-brewing, this usually means a steady temperature of around 65°C (149°F) throughout, though more complex styles and some commercial brewers vary their temperature over the course of the mash. Most mash tuns also have a perforated false bottom and spigot through which the sugary wort passes, leaving the grain in the upper section of the vessel. Once mashing is finished, hot water (usually at around 75°C/167°F) is sprayed over the grains, washing out the dissolved sugars; this is known as sparging or lautering. Throughout this process, it is important for the brewer to maintain the correct density in the mash; if it becomes too dense and begins to press down on the false bottom of the mash tun, its own weight can compress the grains at the bottom, preventing the water from percolating through.

MILK STOUT | STYLE

By the 20th century, stout was essentially being marketed as an energy/health drink for manual workers and the infirm (it was famously given to new mothers after childbirth) and was sometimes even mixed with milk for an extra kick of nutrients and minerals. Milk stout – fortified with unfermentable lactose for a sweet flavour and creamy mouthfeel – was the strange child of this questionable trend. Like so many styles that would otherwise have languished at the back of the beer cellar of history, milk stout has been given a new lease of life by the craft movement (and American brewers in particular), with great beers like Left Hand Milk Stout and Young's Double Chocolate Stout.

MINERALS | SCIENCE

Water always contains a mix of minerals, which varies considerably depending on where in the world you're brewing. As these minerals have a huge impact on a brewer's ability to

SEE ALSO
Lactose p137
Stout p212

M
152

SEE ALSO
Liquor p143
Style p216
Water p231

produce particular styles successfully, it is often necessary to use additional minerals to create a specific water "profile". These are the most common:

- Calcium carbonate, or chalk: raises alkalinity. Add to the mash when making dark beers in areas of soft water.
- Calcium sulfate, or gypsum: raises acidity and adds calcium to water low in sulfate. Lends a certain crispness to hop bitterness.
- Calcium chloride: raises acidity and adds calcium if water is low in chlorides.
- Magnesium sulfate, or Epsom salts: raises acidity slightly, but mostly adds crispness to hops.
- Sodium bicarbonate, or baking soda: raises alkalinity.

There are several websites for brewers that outline the typical water profile of different cities around the world and offer calculators for which minerals to add to achieve different styles.

SEE ALSO
Prohibition *p177*

MONOPOLIES | BEER CULTURE

Usually imposed as a post-Prohibition means of regulating alcohol sales and generally keeping on top of people's drinking habits, several countries still have a state monopoly on the sale of alcohol to private citizens. The Nordic countries are perhaps the best-known example, where, with the exception of Denmark, each country has its own monopoly booze retailer: Systembolaget in Sweden, Alko in Finland, Vínbúð in Iceland and Vinmonopolet in Norway. Canada, too, has state monopolies in every region except Alberta. In complete fairness to the governments of these countries, the state monopolies were generally established in the face of a genuine problem with alcoholism (when it gets that cold, there's not much else to do) and have been both good and bad for the craft beer movement. On the downside, brewers need either to catch the attention of the mighty monopoly (who has bigger fish to fry) or to get really good at selling into bars and restaurants. On the plus side, the monopolies are generally under some obligation to respond to customer demand, they tend to stock a wide selection and, once a brewer has their attention, the orders they place are obviously pretty substantial.

SEE ALSO
Body *p47*
Carbonation *p62*

MOUTHFEEL | TASTING

Similar to body, but somewhat more subjective; literally, the physical sensation of the beer in your mouth. Carbonation is a major part of this: how fizzy is the beer, are the bubbles large or small, how does it prickle your tongue and the roof of your mouth? Body also plays a part: does the beer give your mouth a sense of fullness, does it feel heavy and viscous, or light and thin? Aftertaste is an often neglected element of mouthfeel, but equally important. Does the beer leave you with a mouth-coating roundness, a dry bitterness, stickiness or oiliness? For anyone serious about beer tasting, mouthfeel is as important as flavour and aroma, even if it feels a little pretentious to talk about in the pub or bar.

M
155

NEIPA | STYLE

Whether you prefer the term New England IPA or North East IPA, you're essentially talking about the same thing: the hazy, super-fruity, aromatic-not-bitter, often strong pale ales from (primarily) the northeastern US, most notably from breweries including The Alchemist, Trillium Brewing Company and Treehouse Brewing Company. Often defined in contrast to the crisp, hoppy West Coast IPAs from breweries such as Stone and Ballast Point, NEIPAs have successfully divided the craft beer world between those who see this rule-breaking style as a bold attempt to challenge staid thinking, and those who see it simply as bad brewing.

NEW WORLD HOPS | INGREDIENT

Less a strictly defined category, more a way of differentiating from "Old World" noble hops and their European progeny (presumably borrowing from the New World/Old World distinction in wine). Hop varieties from the Americas, Australia and New Zealand are all usually thrown into this basket and are characterized by their high alpha-acid content and strident aromatic qualities, which often include citrus, mango, pineapple and other juicy fruit. The use of New World hops is one of the signature features of the craft beer movement, or at least was in its early years.

NITROGEN | SCIENCE

SEE ALSO
Draft systems *p77*

Some beers, in particular stouts and most notably Guinness, use nitrogen injection in the draft system to introduce softer effervescence and a creamy mouthfeel, similar to that found in cask ales. The technique requires a special tap at the bar and a mix of carbon dioxide and nitrogen on tank, usually at a ratio of 25:75. Beers destined for a "nitro pour" are specially brewed to have around half the normal amount of carbon dioxide in solution as they leave the brewery; if fully carbonated beer were given a nitro injection it would make a terrible frothy mess. Whereas carbon dioxide dissolves easily in water, nitrogen does not: it tends to escape from solution as soon as it is poured, creating the characteristic creamy foam and cascade of tiny bubbles so beloved of Guinness drinkers. In craft beer circles, stouts served with a nitrogen injection are commonly referred to as "nitro-stout".

NOBLE HOPS | INGREDIENT

SEE ALSO
Britain *p56*
Germany *p99*
Hops *p119*

Four European hop families – Hallertau, Žatec (Saaz), Spalt and Tettnang – used extensively in lagers, pilsners, *dunkels* and *märzens*, as well as many British ales. They are characterized by their relatively low bitterness and high levels of aromatic compounds. There are certain aromas specifically associated with noble hops, including pine, herbs, grass, mint, spice, pepper, flowers and a certain earthiness; they generally lack the fruity notes which characterize many New World hops. Common British descendants of the noble varieties include Fuggles and Goldings.

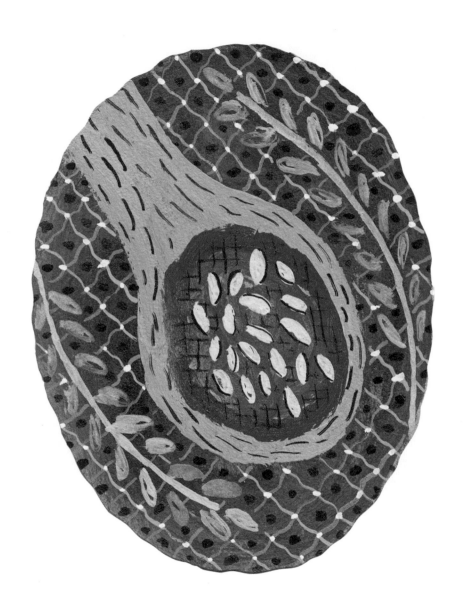

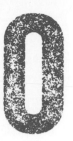

OATS | INGREDIENT

Oats are brimming with antioxidants, proteins, fats, gums and vitamins that create a creamy, full-bodied brew that's silky smooth. They're perfect for stouts or any full-bodied beer. The beta-glucan gums enhance viscosity, which can be good for mouthfeel, but mean that sparging can take up to twice as long for oatmeal stout. The antioxidants may also help protect beers from some problems associated with ageing, and lipids are known to mop up sulfur, an off flavour. Fats have been blamed for poor head retention when oats are added to the grist, though this is more likely to be related to the lower soluble nitrogen content present in worts high in oats, a result of the low nitrogen modification of this grain. It is possible, experimentally, to brew 100 percent oat beer – it smells like berries and yogurt, with butterscotch flavours – but since the high protein and fat content can be difficult to work with, oats normally contribute 5–10 percent of the grist.

O
161

OFF FLAVOURS | FAULT

Flavours and aromas that are broadly agreed to indicate some defect in the brewing. There are many, many things that can go wrong with a brew, from accidental bacterial infection to unhappy yeast, and many of them leave a distinctive tell-tale marker in the finished beer. Apart from under very specific circumstances – if a particular style calls for it, usually – these classic off flavours are considered a serious no-no. Most of the professional beer training programmes, such as Cicerone, include an element of sensory exam, where candidates are required to identify drinks that have been "spiked" with chemicals mimicking off flavours, such an important skill is it considered.

OKTOBERFEST | BEER CULTURE

An annual celebration of beer culture (and Bavarian culture more generally) that has successfully jumped its regional borders, spawning imitators the world over. Referred to colloquially as *Oide Wiesn*, Oktoberfest dates back as far as 1810 and originated as a celebration of the marriage between King Ludwig I of Bavaria to Princess Therese of Saxe-Hildburghausen, though it's changed considerably since then, and grown to welcome around six million people annually. There are several things that mark out Oktoberfest from other popular beer festival formats. First is the selection of beers on offer, or rather the lack of selection: you get a *festbier* and that's generally it. Second, it's served by the litre, in large handled glass mugs known as *maß*, or *mass* (beer geeks take note; many people incorrectly refer to these as "steins", which are actually traditional German stoneware tankards, not glasses). Third, and perhaps most strikingly, most people attending Oktoberfest will be wearing traditional Bavarian dress, so that's lederhosen for the boys and a dirndl for the girls. Finally, the whole affair is soundtracked by a Bavarian "oom-pah" brass band, usually playing a mix

SEE ALSO
Festivals *p88*
Germany *p99*
Lager (definition 1) *p138*

O
162

of modern favourites and traditional drinking songs (and woe to anyone who fails to stand and take a hearty swig from their *maß* at the appropriate moment in these numbers).

OXIDATION | FAULT

SEE ALSO
Off flavours *p161*

Chemical reactions arising from exposure to air, either in individual ingredients before brewing or in the beer itself. Oxidation is, without wishing to overdramatize things, the arch-nemesis of beer, responsible for a whole host of off flavours:

- Stale, wet paper or cardboard: often found in overboiled beers, old (as opposed to deliberately aged) beers and even beers that have just been left open too long. If you've ever thought it would be a great idea to sample the dregs of last night's beer the next day, then you'll know this one.
- Leather, tobacco: this arises from the oxidation of malt compounds and is quite distinctive. In fresh beers, it's definitely to be avoided, but in older aged beers can give interesting layers of additional character.
- Honey, beeswax: great in honey beers (please don't send your honey beer back if it tastes of honey), but in anything else a sure sign of oxidation and staleness, particularly in lagers and pilsners.

PALE ALE | STYLE

While pale ale has become a style in its own right in the craft world – and is usually associated with strong, hoppy ales – it has traditionally encompassed a range of related beers, including IPA and various English bitters. The latter are often given the prefixes "ordinary", "best", "special" and "extra special" as an indicator of their relative alcoholic strength. Pale ale and IPA (or, at least, the traditional English versions of these styles, as opposed to their US counterparts) have few meaningful differences from English bitter, except that they tend to be at the stronger end of the ABV range, with a pronounced bitterness to match. The town of Burton upon Trent became the spiritual home of English pale ales, as the mineral content of the water there is perfect for this style. They're all based on pale ale malt, which gives a crisp but slightly nutty malt profile, and often use adjuncts, including flaked barley and wheat, to help with head retention and mouthfeel.

PASTEUR, LOUIS | SCIENCE

Microbiologist and chemist Louis Pasteur is without doubt one of the great unsung heroes of brewing history. Not only did he contribute the process of sterilization which bears his name (pasteurization), he also greatly advanced our understanding of the role of yeast in fermentation, as well as correctly identifying that lactic acid formation was the result of a different microorganism, essentially paving the way for modern, controlled brewing. Pasteur's interest in fermentation began in 1856, when a local winemaker – whose son was a student of Pasteur's in Lille – asked for his advice on a problem he was experiencing with souring. Over the following years, Pasteur's experiments proved that yeast, not decomposition, was responsible for fermentation, and that the contamination and growth of other microorganisms were responsible for spoiling. Armed with this knowledge, he created his eponymous process for sterilizing liquids, which involved heating them to 60–100°C (140–212°F), thereby killing off any bugs that might already be present. It was this work in alcohol production that eventually led Pasteur to theorize that microorganism infection might also be responsible for many human diseases – an idea that would prompt Joseph Lister to propose sterile surgical processes a couple of years later, in 1867. Brewing is therefore, in a very real sense, the cornerstone on which all modern medicine sits. Probably.

PEDIOCOCCUS | SCIENCE

A bacterium found on plants and fruit that produces lactic acid and diacetyl. A crucial part of the flavour profile of lambic and *gueuze*, it is otherwise a major headache for commercial brewers, as infections take a lot of cleaning and sterilization to eradicate. *Pediococcus* is also the most common cause of "ropiness" (sometimes called "sick beer"), a condition that causes

the beer to become viscous and, in extreme circumstances, form gelatinous, rope-like strands. These will usually dissolve in time, but are nonetheless gross.

pH | SCIENCE

A measure of the acidity or alkalinity of a solution, on a scale ranging from 0 (very acid) to 14 (very alkaline), with 7 being neutral. The pH of water is very important at each step of the brewing process, and in the final beer. At mashing, the water should be between 5.2 and 5.5, as the all-important alpha- and beta-amylase enzymes don't work well outside of this range and will eventually be destroyed by anything too extreme. In wort, pH is important in creating the right conditions for proteins to join together, while in fermentation it has a big impact on the health and behaviour of yeast. The final pH of beer usually falls somewhere between 4 and 5, though in sour beers it can be lower. Brewers can alter the pH of their brews by adding certain minerals to their brewing liquor.

PHENOLS | SCIENCE

A class of chemical compounds found in many beers, arising from a number of sources which, like esters, can be a virtue or a vice, depending on their concentration and the style of the beer. When drinkers say a beer tastes "phenolic", they're usually picking up on the presence of aromatic volatile phenols. These stand out like a sore thumb even in very small quantities, and manifest themselves as clovey, medicinal or smoky aromas. Phenols are sometimes already present in the brewing water or the malt. With a smoked beer like a *rauchbier*, a phenolic tang from the smoked malt is clearly an integral part of the style. Chlorine used in water treatment can encourage higher levels of phenols if not removed, and is usually characterized by an antiseptic, iodine aroma. Phenols can also be a by-product of yeast, where they often appear as clove-like notes. This is a familiar flavour and aroma to anyone acquainted with German wheat beers and many Belgian ales, and brewers of these styles actively encourage the development of these phenols during fermentation.

PILOT BREWING | BEER CULTURE

SEE ALSO
Brewhouse p55

When breweries reach a certain scale, it becomes tricky for them to experiment with new styles and ingredients, partly because it takes capacity away from main production, but also because the size of their brewhouse means that if an experimental beer doesn't work out, they are suddenly stuck with a *lot* of bad beer. To get around this, many breweries keep a "pilot" kit, a vastly scaled down version of their production brew kit, roughly equivalent to what a particularly well-resourced home-brewer might have in their garage. As many craft brewers once *were* home-brewers, their pilot kit is frequently the equipment on which they originally honed their craft. So if you see, tucked away in the corner of the brewery, a weird mishmash of brewing vessels on borrowed wheels, held together by an uneasy coalition of amateur welding, duct tape and prayer, it is probably the brewer's beloved pilot kit.

PILSNER | STYLE

As a style, pilsner – a member of the lager family – originated in the Czech town of Plzeň or Pilsen in 1842 and has spawned imitators all over the

world. When it's good, it's great, with plenty of caramel malt in the shadow of fresh and spicy Saaz hops; when it's bad (as it often is), it can be pretty two-dimensional, particularly on the hop front. German brewers adopted the style a little later and tweaked it slightly; German pilsners tend to be drier, with a more herbal and overtly bitter hop profile.

SEE ALSO
Malts, colour *p148*
Stout *p212*

PORTER | STYLE

The uneasy truth (particularly in a dictionary) is that nobody wants to say definitively what a porter is, or when and where it was invented, and I'm certainly not about to start here. What we can say with some certainty is that it evolved independently out of several varieties of brown ale, emerging as a dark (but certainly not black) nutty beer popular among the transport workers from whom it takes its name. At first it would have been brewed predominantly from heavily kilned "brown" malt, giving it a rich flavour, deep malty aroma and full body. However, brewers quickly realized this was a *horribly* inefficient way to brew, as these malts (while delicious) provided very little fermentable sugar. At around the beginning of the 19th century porter started to be brewed with higher-yielding pale base malt and coloured deep brown with whatever vile additives the brewers could lay their hands on. This sorry state of affairs ended around 15 years later, when it was discovered that roasting malt to a deep, dark black imparted a huge amount of colour and even some chocolate/coffee characteristics in relatively small amounts. Modern porters are rich in roasted and toasted malt flavour and aroma, with plenty of hop bitterness but little hop aroma; they often have a medium body and mouthfeel.

P

POURING | DRINKING

Serving a great pint, whether at home or at the bar, is almost a shibboleth among beer lovers. The last thing you want to hear from a friend, when pouring a can of the latest and greatest, is "Can I have a flake with that, please?" The best way to achieve a good firm head – not too tall, not too feeble – is a matter of some contention, though. If you're at home and time is on your side, the consensus is that it's best to pour the beer directly into the bottom of the glass, creating an enormous head, which you then leave to settle before repeating until the glass is full. The logic is that this creates a much thicker, creamier foam. Your hypothetical friend may well have got fed up by this point, though, and gently suggested you stop being such an insufferable beer bore and just pour the damn drink. In which case, you will probably want to go with the more expedient pub or bar technique, angling the glass at 45 degrees and pouring the beer steadily down the inside until it is roughly two-thirds full, then straightening it up to allow the final third to form a head.

PROGRESSIVE BEER DUTY | BEER CULTURE

A system of duty relief to encourage the growth of small brewers. The idea originated in Bavaria and was subsequently adopted by the European Union as an optional structure for member states. It is implemented in slightly different ways depending on the country, but generally breweries receive a 50 percent discount on duty up to a certain annual volume: a discount that decreases in steps as the brewery's output grows. This policy has arguably played a major role in the evolution of craft beer in some countries. It has, however, drawn the criticism that it

provides a strong disincentive for breweries to grow over a certain size, and has stifled acquisitions among medium-sized breweries.

PROHIBITION | BEER CULTURE

Many societies have, at one time or another, attempted to prohibit or at least severely curtail the production, sale and consumption of alcohol, either out of concern for the health of their citizenry or out of religious doctrine or moral squeamishness. While some such regimes are still in place, they have generally failed or are at least easily circumvented by those with a will to drink. The most famous programme of prohibition was America's own "Noble Experiment"; this began in 1919, when the manufacture, distribution and sale of alcohol were made illegal for all those without a special medicinal licence. The ban was enacted in response to waves of social upheaval in the wake of the industrial revolution, when crime, alcoholism and a host of other social ills all spiked. However good its intentions, Prohibition turned out to be a flop, shifting the lucrative alcohol industry away from law-abiding, tax-paying employers into the hands of criminal gangs for whom bootlegging and smuggling became a major new revenue stream. When Franklin Roosevelt stood for the presidency promising a repeal of the Prohibition laws, he won one of the biggest landslides in American history, and the Noble Experiment was abandoned in 1933.

PUB | DRINKING

Pubs, taverns and inns are a cornerstone of western social history, taking root in a huge

SEE ALSO
Monopolies p154

SEE ALSO
Taproom p219

number of countries and providing a focal point for communities, a vital social arena and even a place of business and commerce. Before the 20th century, going to the pub was pretty much the only thing to do outside of work and home for the working and lower-middle classes. In the run-up to the industrial revolution, the inn was a conduit for people, money and goods that facilitated economic growth. It was also the place for political movements to galvanize, and many a revolution – some more successful than others – was fomented over the beer-saturated sawdust of a tavern floor. The pub was not just home to relaxing manual labourers and would-be radicals, however. For many artisan workers, the pub was both their living room and a marketplace, with the chance to pick up passing trade or even forge local relationships for long-term custom. Lawyers might set up office in the "snug", a small, very private room useful for confidentiality, and also used by those who did not wish to be seen in the public bar (the off-duty policeman, perhaps, or the local vicar sneaking a cheeky sherry). The traditional pub has also hosted a huge range of popular recreations across time, from cock-fighting to gooseberry shows, dancing girls and the skittle alley, the pub quiz and the terror-inducing karaoke night.

The business of the 21st-century pub has changed, of course, going through many modern-day evolutions and permutations – from food-centric "gastropubs" to the more casual bar favoured in North America – but never quite being killed off. With pubs closing at a rate of knots in some countries it might seem that they have finally lost their raison d'être. Yet the rise and rise of micropubs and brewery taprooms is testament to the fact that pubs can rediscover (or even reinvent) themselves. Vital village pubs

take up the slack left by culled local services, becoming the local post office, farmer's shop and makeshift library; the only place that has a decent internet connection. Especially in these rural areas, you'll still find a congregation of habitués, seeking the security of a warm, familiar roof over their heads and a beer.

PUMPKIN ALE | STYLE

....

While craft beer's contribution to the sum of human happiness and beauty has generally been positive, the creation of pumpkin ale falls firmly into the "debit" column of the ledger. Arising first in the US, this seasonal autumnal beer uses roasted pumpkin (usually in the boil, sometimes in the mash – it's surprisingly contentious) to add flavour and fermentable sugar. Where these beers often go wrong is in letting the vegetable sweetness of the pumpkin overpower the more subtle, nuanced character of the malt. Brewers also have a tendency to load them up with seasonally appropriate spices such as cinnamon and cloves, making a wild, unbalanced mess of flavours and aromas.

SEE ALSO
Boil *p48*
Mash *p151*
Festive ale *p91*

QA | BEER CULTURE

These days, even the smallest craft breweries tend to have some sort of quality assurance (QA) regime in place, scaling right up to well-equipped on-site laboratories. As well as ensuring there are no technical faults with the beer, QA is about keeping brews consistent over time, monitoring their shelf life and other broader quality issues. Most breweries will keep back a small supply from each batch they brew for this purpose. In addition to sophisticated equipment for measuring every chemical variable of the beer, qualitative testing – in which expert human tasters give their verdict – is used to assess whether or not a beer is up to scratch.

RADLERS AND SHANDIES | STYLE

SEE ALSO
Cocktails *p66*

Mixes of beer with non-alcoholic soda or fruit juice; either ale (usually bitter) or lager can be used for the purpose. There are many specific variations, such as the Diesel (*Düsseldorfer Altbier* and cola). Every now and then, somebody decides artisanal shandies and radlers are going to be the next big thing in craft beer, though they have so far been unswervingly wrong. There are a number of other mixes which, while not strictly shandies, work in a similar way. Snakebite is a mix of beer and cider, while the infamous turbo shandy is a particularly classy blend of beer and alcoholic/hard lemonade.

RATEBEER | BEER CULTURE

SEE ALSO
Untappd *p227*

Ratebeer.com has become a hugely important part of the craft beer world. Essentially a ratings site, it invites individual users to score and write tasting notes for every beer they try. In an often confusing marketplace, this kind of collective rating has become a vital navigational aid. It has also spawned a subculture in its own right: go to any major beer festival and you are likely to see a table or two covered in notes, score sheets, Post-it Notes and many, many empty glasses. This is the Ratebeer crowd, and the earnest-looking folk who make up its ranks take their self-appointed job very seriously, with the most prolific reviewers rising to something like celebrity status.

RAUCHBIER | STYLE

SEE ALSO
Phenols *p169*

Throughout most of Europe, smoked beers were ditched pretty much as soon as we figured out how to build indirect kilns, and were able to dry malt without exposing it to smoke (this happened around 1700). One of the very few exceptions to this was in a region of northern Bavaria, around Bamberg, where they elected to carry on brewing with their smoky malts, and do to this day. *Rauchbier* is almost a technique rather than a specific style, in which unsmoked malt is simply substituted with the smoked equivalent for a range of different lagers, primarily *märzen*, *helles*, *bock* and *weizen* – basically, any lager style with enough malty clout to stand up to a layer of sweet, bacony beech wood. Needless to say, this sort of mucking about with lagers divides opinions sharply, even if it does have sound historical precedent.

REAL ALE | STYLE

SEE ALSO
Britain *p56*
CAMRA *p61*
Cask *p65*
Macro-brewing *p145*

R
184

The crown jewel of the UK's brewing tradition, even if its relationship with the nation's burgeoning craft beer scene is, at times, a little antagonistic. CAMRA, the custodian, saviour and cheerleader of this tradition, defines real ale as "a natural product brewed using traditional ingredients and left to mature in the cask from which it is served in the pub through a process called secondary fermentation". In other words, real ale consists of super-traditional British styles, shipped out in casks while they are still fermenting. Once the norm in pubs,

inns and taverns across the land, real ale is now definitely a speciality, and maintaining a cellar is considered a genuine skill. The cask itself has two openings: one at the head, in which a plug called the keystone is placed, and another on the broadest point of the side, where the unfinished ale is filled and stoppered with a wooden plug called a shive. When it reaches the pub cellar, the cask is stored on its side with the shive facing upward, and a porous peg called a spile is driven into the shive to vent any excess carbon dioxide over the course of a day or two. Once the cellar master determines that the beer has reached its prime, the porous spile is replaced with a hard peg so the cask retains its pressure. It is then left for a couple more days to allow yeast and other solids to drop out of suspension and fall to the bottom of the cask, leaving the beer clear and bright (as all cask ales should be). Once it's ready to be served, a tap is deftly hammered into the keystone (trickier than it looks) and the beer can begin to flow. After a cask of real ale has been tapped, it's only a matter of days before oxygen and airborne mircroorganisms begin to do their work and the beer spoils. This is why stock management is as crucial a part of running a successful real-ale pub as technical cask management.

REINHEITSGEBOT | BEER CULTURE

With roots dating back 500 years, to a decree by Wilhelm IV, Duke of Bavaria, the German *Reinheitsgebot* or "purity law" today mandates that anything sold as beer in Germany must comprise only four ingredients: malted barley, hops, yeast and water. The original text didn't mention yeast, as it hadn't been discovered at that time, and was actually more concerned with standardizing and limiting the cost of beer than it was about ingredients. While some in Germany now believe the law should be relaxed, it remains the foundation of the country's global reputation for quality and precision in beer making, and has been adopted voluntarily by Teutophile brewers all over the world.

RELIGION | BEER CULTURE

Beer and religion have a long and often antagonistic relationship going back thousands of years, from ancient deities to Trappist brewers and the modern temperance movement. Most cultures have alcohol somewhere in their mythology, whether it's the Sumerians' beer goddess Ninkasi, Roman good-time god Bacchus (or Dionysus if the ancient Greeks are more to your taste), the Norse pantheon's party-giving Aegir or even Christianity's wine-based holy communion. There are, however, just as many scriptural warnings against the vices of alcohol, with some religions going so far as to prohibit booze completely; many modern secular movements to curb alcohol abuse (such as Alcoholics Anonymous in the US) are underpinned by a distinctly (and sometimes overtly) religious sense of morality.

RICE | INGREDIENT

Generally used in brewing simply to add cheap fermentable sugars, rather than for flavour or aroma (though some varieties of rice can add character too). Like corn, it must be gelatinized by boiling before being added to the mash. Rice is a common ingredient in mass-produced American light lagers. Rice hulls – the protective covering of the rice grain – are more often used

SEE ALSO
Trappist *p223*

SEE ALSO
Adjunct *p14*
American lager *p20*
Aroma *p23*
Mash *p151*
Stuck sparge *p215*

R

in all-grain home-brewing circles, as their
addition to the mash can help prevent the mass
of grain becoming too dense, thereby avoiding
the dreaded stuck sparge.

RYE | INGREDIENT

A perfect partner for barley, and particularly
useful for adding complexity and crispness.
Spicy rye lends a keen, dry bite to lagers and
can be kilned to create chocolate and caramel
versions. Colour-wise, a rye beer will have a
luxurious, red autumnal hue. A rye IPA tends
to have a sharp edge and a crisp, distinctive
finish leaning toward apple brandy. Rye's major
shortcoming is that it can turn to concrete
during brewing, because it has no hull to keep
the grains apart and is high in sticky beta-glucan
gums. Typically, a 10 percent grist works well,
though the German-style *Roggenbiers* have a
mash bill of at least 30 percent rye and some up to
65 percent, giving them a sharp rye flavour and
medium-heavy mouthfeel.

R
101

SAISON | STYLE

A style whose roots are shrouded in the mists of rural history but which, legend has it, was brewed to quench the thirst of farmhands and seasonal workers in the heat of the Belgian summer. Today's *saison* can range in strength from a light session ale to around 10 percent ABV. Malt is light and clean with a hint of caramel and well balanced by peppery, fresh noble hops on a super-dry base. The yeast character dominates, though, and can often be quite phenolic and spicy (some brewers even add spice to complement this character), sometimes with a note of tangy fruit. It's a broad style, so you'll occasionally even catch a farmyard whiff of *Brettanomyces* in there for good measure.

SANITIZATION | BREWING

Is not the same as cleaning. In cleaning, we ensure equipment or glassware isn't dirty; in sanitization, we ensure it's free from harmful microbes that could spoil the beer. For brewing equipment, there are special non-detergent sanitization products designed to foam up then break down into compounds that will not taint the beer or be harmful to yeast health. In bars, a suds-free sanitizer is used at the end of preparing a glass for use, ensuring it is "beer clean".

SEE ALSO
Glassware *p99*

SCHOONER | DRINKING

....

Winning the award for most confusing serving size, a "schooner" lacks legal definition and will generally get you something quite different depending on where in the world you happen to ask. In Southern Australia it's half an imperial pint (285ml), whereas elsewhere in the country it generally means 425ml, or three-quarters of an imperial pint. In Canada, it's even less consistent, referring simply to a large glass, though the most common size is around two US pints (950ml). In the US, a schooner is more about shape than capacity: rounded, with a stem, and weighing in at anything from 1.1–2 pints (530–950ml). In the UK, a schooner started out as a large sherry glass, though in the beer world it now generally means 379ml or two-thirds of a pint, unless you're in the city of Newcastle, where it traditionally means a half-pint glass. Clear? No? Me neither.

SCOTTISH ALES | STYLE

....

SEE ALSO
Wee heavy *p232*

Somewhat similar to their English counterparts, with a couple of notable styles all of their own. The strength of Scottish beers has historically been designated by "shillings" (an obsolete British unit of currency) – indicative of the cost of a barrel of the stuff at some long-forgotten point in the past. Although such a measure is pretty meaningless these days, the tradition has stuck, and Caledonian 80 shilling (80/- or just "Cal 80") is a common sight behind many an Edinburgh pub bar, as well as being an excellent example of the style. In medieval times, malted barley would have been dried over peat fires, giving it a distinctive smoky, phenolic character, as is still the case with whiskies in some parts

of the country. These days, there are no such smoky notes in traditional Scottish beer, unless they're added for the tourists. Having been largely confined to Scotland's rocky shores in the past, several styles have recently found favour among international craft brewers, including Scotch ale and wee heavy: strong, heavy, barley wines that are particularly suitable for barrel-ageing.

SCOTTISH EXPORT | STYLE

A more interesting beast than the light and heavy ales, the export-strength 80 shilling (80/-) ales are more similar to a good English pale ale or bitter. Hop aroma still takes a back seat, but there is a definite bitterness to this style, giving depth to the complex toffee and toasty malt. Good examples include Belhaven Scottish Ale and McEwan's Export.

SCOTTISH HEAVY | STYLE

Sometimes called 70 shilling (70/-), this is a light session ale, coming in at 3.5–4 percent ABV. With a very similar character to Scottish light ale, it has no real hop aroma, but a slightly creamier, more complex malt base.

SCOTTISH LIGHT ALE | STYLE

Often given the designation 60 shilling (60/-), Scottish light ale is broadly analogous to English bitter, with a clean malt character, no hop aroma to speak of and hints of caramel on the nose. Weighing in at around 3 percent ABV, this isn't a style you see much of in the wild any more.

SEE ALSO
Ale *p17*
Pale ale *p165*

SEE ALSO
Scottish Light Ale *p197*

SECONDARY FERMENTATION | BREWING

A blanket term for the various processes of additional fermentation and conditioning that take place after primary fermentation (the active period when the bulk of the fermentable sugar is converted to alcohol and carbon dioxide) is complete, but before the beer has been entirely removed from the yeast. In lagers (including pilsners, *kölsches* and so on) secondary fermentation takes place during the "lagering" phase, which can last many weeks. In this cold, slow secondary fermentation, the remaining yeast in suspension continues its work, bringing about important chemical changes in the beer, most notably mopping up any remaining diacetyl. In ale brewing, secondary fermentation often means allowing carbon dioxide to dissolve in the beer, giving it a gentle sparkle (as opposed to the stronger fizz of forced carbonation) as well as removing unwanted flavour compounds. This conditioning process happens either in conditioning tanks or, in the case of traditional English ales, in a bottle or cask.

SELLING OUT | BEER CULTURE

As the craft beer movement has matured across the world, those of us cheering from the sidelines have been forced to reconcile ourselves to the fact that the scrappy young breweries we so badly wanted to succeed might, at some point, do just that. Sometimes they get slick in their marketing, start opening in other locations and sell their beer in supermarkets. They might even sell all or part of their business, perhaps even to one of the phenomenally well-resourced macro-breweries we're all supposed to hate. This is like seeing Peter Pan take a job as a loss adjuster, and it makes

otherwise decent people confused and angry. But is it really all that bad? It gives the craft brewery new opportunities to spread its gospel to an even wider audience and is an acknowledgment that, just maybe, we were right about this stuff all along. Plus, on a purely materialistic level, who are we to tell brewers who have toiled at the mash tun for 20-plus years that they don't deserve their windfall?

SERVERS | DRINKING

What makes a great beer bar? Having 40 lines of fresh brews from the best breweries across the world certainly helps. A live DJ or jazz trio, depending on your taste, will definitely add to the atmosphere. Home-made bar snacks are a nice touch. But it's really the expertise and commitment of the folk behind the bar that will keep you coming back. No longer is it acceptable for a beer server to answer "I don't know" if you ask "What's that one like?", and try-before-you-buy is simply good manners. Fortunately, good independent pubs, bars and taprooms are in the ascendancy, and internationally recognized beer training schemes – such as those run by Cicerone and the Munich-based Doemens – provide an easy way to get servers up to speed with their knowledge of styles, character and the technical aspects of serving a perfect pint.

SEE ALSO
Draft systems *p77*
Keggerator *p134*

SERVING TEMPERATURE | DRINKING

An often-neglected factor in the enjoyment of beer. After all the trouble that goes into brewing a beer, with flavour, aroma, mouthfeel, body, carbonation and a host of other variables all in perfect balance, serving it at an inappropriate temperature can still kill the experience. This is as much a problem in many bars as it is at home;

in both settings, all styles are often served at the same extreme chill that you might serve a lager, leaving most aromas sitting inert in the glass and numbing the tongue to all those wonderful nuances of flavour. The range of ideal serving temperatures is surprisingly broad – from 3–13°C (37–55°F) – so it's worth at least trying to get it into the right ballpark. While tradition dictates certain specific temperatures for certain styles, two good rules of thumb are 1) beers fermented at low temperatures should be served at low temperatures; and 2) the darker the beer, the higher the ideal serving temperature. Beer packaging will often recommend a serving temperature, but in broad terms continental lagers and pilsners should be at 3–7°C (37–45°F), light speciality ales at 4–10°C (39–50°F), dark ales at 7–13°C (45–55°F) and real ale at cellar temperature, 10–13°C (50–55°F).

SESSION BEERS | STYLE

Designed, as the name suggests, for a steady afternoon or evening's drinking, without you ending up incoherent in a bus shelter. Not only are session beers relatively low in ABV (which should mean less than 4 percent, but in craft circles can creep higher), but they should also be of a palatable bitterness, aromatic and generally pleasant to to keep drinking for a prolonged period. Session beers are not a style in their own right, though are usually lighter beers, predominantly IPAs and pale ales. Good examples include Founders All Day IPA, Stone Go To IPA and Beavertown Neck Oil. Although it seems to be a relatively modern term, there is speculation that its roots are in post-war Britain, when pubs were restricted to opening during two tightly controlled afternoon and evening "sessions".

SEE ALSO
ABV *p13*
IPA *p128*
Pale ale *p165*

SHELF LIFE | TASTING

Particularly in the modern era of global beer distribution, shelf life is a hugely important characteristic and – sadly – continues to be a real challenge in the world of craft beer. Some styles are inevitably more "shelf stable" than others, as an immutable fact of chemistry. Those which rely on hop aroma, for example, tend to be best super-fresh, as the essential oils that impart the characteristic juicy tropical fruit notes tend to break down very quickly. The same is true of many fruit beers, though it also depends on the fruit being used. Poor shelf stability can be down to faults in brewing or packaging, too. Rigorous filtering undoubtedly extends shelf life, but isn't always desirable as it can mean compromising on flavour and mouthfeel. The opposite is also true, though: leaving compounds in the brew that arguably shouldn't be there can drastically increase the chances of a beer going bad rapidly. This is why hazy, soupy NEIPAs tend not to travel so well. Shelf life is always shortened by mistreatment of the beer between the brewery and the glass – for example, by exposure to heat or, in the case of bottled beers, excessive light. While they are a lot more expensive, beers such as American IPAs are increasingly being shipped in refrigerated containers so they never have even the briefest opportunity to warm up.

SIEBEL INSTITUTE, THE | BEER CULTURE

The oldest and probably best-known brewing school in the US, the Siebel Institute of Technology (originally called the Zymotechnic Institute) was founded in Chicago in 1868 by a German immigrant, John Ewald Siebel.

He began teaching brewing classes there in 1882, but it wasn't until his sons joined the business in the 1890s that these classes became a major, regular part of the institute's activities. A full range of classes continues to be taught at the institute's home in Chicago, as well as at several other sites. Siebel is also extremely active in brewing research, particularly in the area of fermentation science.

SINGLE-HOP BEERS | STYLE

An increasingly popular way of brewing in the US and UK, single-hop beers showcase the characteristics of just one hop variety for bittering and aroma. Drinkers are able to identify and learn about the unique characteristics of that hop, potentially allowing them to pick it out in other beers containing multiple varieties. Single-hop beers also play well to ideas of locality and seasonality, which are becoming ever more important among craft beer fans.

SNACKS | DRINKING

The availability and nature of bar snacks tells beer lovers a great deal about the kind of establishment they're drinking in. Bowls of dusty beer nuts, for example, suggest that some knowledge of football would be socially useful. Pork scratchings or beef jerky are one step up the ladder, while the fairly recent advent of wasabi peas indicate that the landlord is sick of his elderly regulars nursing a single pint all evening and yearns for an edgier clientele. Kilner jars of artisan-pickled root vegetables and sourdough mean you might want to consider taking out a mortgage before buying a pint.

SOUR | STYLE

The term "sour" beer covers a multitude of styles and techniques – so many in fact that it is considered by some pundits to be rather unhelpful, in that it invites comparison between beers that set out to be quite different from one another. What they have in common, though, is a tart sourness (rather than bitterness – a distinction which confuses a lot of beer novices). The simplest way of making a beer sour is to raise its base acidity using *Lactobacillus* bacteria when mashing in the grains. This technique, known as kettle souring, adds only 48 hours to a beer's production time and is pretty safe and predictable. Mixed fermentation uses a mixture of yeast and bacteria; these beers take significantly longer than kettle souring and are considerably more expensive to make. As well as the more complex (often slower) primary fermentation, mixed and spontaneously fermented beers are frequently left in wooden barrels for a year or more in order to fully mature.

SPARGE | BREWING

Also called lautering, sparging is a vital stage in the brewing process, wherein sugars are washed from the mash using a steady flow of hot liquor; the resulting sweet, malty liquid is called wort. Most mash tuns have a perforated false bottom with a spigot underneath, so the brewer can catch the runoff from the mash and transfer it to the boiling vessel. The most common sparging technique is the continuous sparge, in which water is sprayed slowly over the top of the mash tun; as it percolates down between the grains, the water increases in sugar concentration. The initial runoff usually contains some husks and other unwanted particles, so this is often passed back to the top of the mash tun and through the grain bed, which then acts as a filter. Too fast or too slow a sparge can lead to compression of the grain bed, and the dreaded "stuck" sparge.

SPENT GRAIN | BREWING

The crushed husks and other debris left over after mashing and sparging have extracted most of the carbohydrates from the grain. This is often simply discarded, though environmentally conscientious modern brewers are increasingly looking to reduce their waste footprint by finding other uses for their spent grain. Rural breweries often donate theirs to nearby farms, as it makes excellent cattle feed, while some innovative companies have even started using it to make cereal bars for human consumption. Spent grain, by the way, is referred to as "draff" in the whisky world, and I've never been sure why this hasn't caught on in beer. It's a wonderful word.

SPONTANEOUS FERMENTATION | BREWING

The fermentation of beer not through deliberate addition of specific yeast or bacterial strains, but by allowing naturally occurring microorganisms in the environment (either airborne or, more commonly now, already present in the fermentation vessels) to infect the wort. This is a feature of many styles, but is particularly associated with "wild" sour beers, such as lambic and Flanders red. Spontaneous fermentation can be unpredictable and is always considerably slower than conventional fermentation with brewer's yeast.

STEPPED MASH | BREWING

At its most basic, mashing just involves adding grain to water at a certain temperature and maintaining that temperature for a set amount of time. However, as the various enzyme groups involved in the process each have their own optimum temperature, some brewers use "step mashing" or "upward step mash" to achieve specific effects. These more sophisticated mashing programmes could include just a couple of steps or, for some styles, many small steps, taking the mash all the way from room temperature to boiling point. Continental European brewing traditions are most closely associated with stepped mashing, and many Belgian styles require it. Perhaps the most complex mashing technique, though, is the German "decoction", in which a portion of the mash is removed, briefly boiled and returned to the mash tun, raising the temperature of the whole. This can be repeated two or three times over the course of several hours.

STORAGE | TASTING

Although much depends on style, beer is generally pretty delicate, and sensitive to being kept in the wrong environment. Particularly if it's a beer with a very limited shelf life, or one that you intend to age, having the right conditions is essential. Unless it's cask beer, which is deliberately sent out into the world still fermenting, breweries will only sell "finished" beer, but this does not mean it is completely inert. Far from it, in fact; significant changes can take place in the bottle, altering or completely ruining the beer's character. Flavours, particularly from fruit or zingy aromatic hops, lose their impact (which is why the only place to enjoy a US-style West Coast pale ale is on the West Coast), oxidation sets in and the proteins, which have so much impact on mouthfeel and head retention, begin to break down and sink despondently to the bottom of the bottle.

Temperature is the main factor, as heat will accelerate the chemical reactions that bring about these unwanted changes. Fluctuations between hot and cold aren't great either, so once a beer is in the fridge, try to leave it there unless you intend to drink it. Finally, light is definitely to be avoided. While brown bottles give good protection against beer-destroying ultraviolet rays, a beer left in direct sunlight for weeks on end will still suffer. In summary then: store in a cool, dark, dry place.

As a small caveat to the idea that breweries sell only finished beer, there seems to be a trend developing for selling bottles with the recommendation that they are not ready to drink straight away, but should be left to mature in a cool, dark place. This seems to be the brewing equivalent of "ripen at home" supermarket fruit and, one can only hope, will prove to be a passing fad.

STOUT | STYLE

Ireland caught the dark beer bug from England at exactly the time that porter really started taking off, at the tail end of the 19th century. From that point, though, the two traditions followed rather different paths. Irish stout is distinct in its use of roasted barley (as opposed to the black roasted malt of English porter), which gives it a signature coffee sharpness. A quantity of unmalted barley is also commonly included in

SEE ALSO
Porter *p173*

the mash bill, giving stout a smoother, creamier mouthfeel. Stout has historically been brewed slightly stronger than porters, though trends in craft beer have seen a strong resurgence in the former, which is now being brewed at ever-stronger ABVs.

STRENGTH | BEER CULTURE

SEE ALSO
ABV p13
Alcohol p16
Style p216

For years, alcoholic strength was seen by the majority simply as a measure of how quickly beer would get you drunk. With craft, though, we have rediscovered that strength is also an important aspect of style, working in harmony with other elements of character, including malt, bitterness, aroma, body, carbonation and mouthfeel. For example, a classic lager simply wouldn't work at 8 percent, whereas a 4 percent English barley wine would seem unbearably sweet and cloying.

STUCK SPARGE | FAULT

SEE ALSO
Home-brew p113
Mash p151
Wort p240

The bane of many a home-brewer, and one of the most common mistakes you can make. It occurs when the grain bed and filter become too dense or clogged for liquor to flow through it slows to a trickle and then stops, leaving you wondering what on earth to do next.

Some grains, such as wheat, are more prone to causing a stuck sparge than others, so take this into account when creating a recipe. Prevention is better than cure, and including a small quantity of rice hulls in your mash bill will help, as will keeping the temperature up (if the grains get too cold they become gelatinous and stick together) and making sure your grain isn't crushed too finely.

STYLE | STYLE

Particularly in the world of craft beer, where new and disruptive thinking is seen as a virtue, style is a tricky beast. It is arguably the cornerstone of beer appreciation, allowing us not only to understand what we're ordering, but also to judge whether it has been brewed successfully. Each style is a collection of characteristics, history and commonly held understandings that coalesce into an often nebulous picture of what a beer means and how it should be interpreted by the brewer and the drinkers. Styles often overlap, or diverge sharply from their own history, coming to mean different things in different parts of the world over time. We of course try to pin this unwieldy mess down into something a little more objective, through style guides and competition judging criteria, though even this idea – that there might be a definitive "right" way to brew a particular style – has only really emerged in the past 50 years.

Craft brewers on the one hand seem to respect the idea of style – insofar as it encourages discipline and brewing to a particular purpose – yet on the other hand constantly challenge it with hybrid brews, unusual additions and occasionally even deliberate off flavours, so expect the unexpected.

SUPERTASTERS | DRINKING

A genetic quirk which gives around 20 percent of us (with a slight bias toward women) an exceptionally sensitive palate, particularly when it comes to bitterness. As mutant superpowers go, this one isn't going to be much use in fighting crime, but it certainly makes a difference to your taste in beer. At the other end of the scale are

those poor unfortunates (around 40 percent) labelled non-tasters; this doesn't mean they can't taste anything, but rather that they are significantly less sensitive. Those of us in the remaining 40 percent wonder what all the fuss is about and continue to knock back our alpha acid-laden DIPAs with wild abandon.

T-SHIRTS | BEER CULTURE

SEE ALSO
Artwork *p24*

It's hard to overstate the cultural importance of T-shirts in the world of craft beer. They're not only a way to show allegiance to a favourite brewery; they're also powerful status symbols, with iconic, obscure or overseas breweries sure to earn the admiration of one's peers. In the US you will often see a brewer visiting a neighbouring brewery, wearing the T-shirt of a mutually respected third brewery. Such is the complicated social dance of beer-related merchandise.

TAPROOM | DRINKING

SEE ALSO
Brewpub *p56*
Pub *p177*

A beer-focused bar, usually on the site of – or at least closely associated with – a particular craft brewery. Originally an American innovation, taprooms have quickly taken off elsewhere, and their success is generally beating the trend in an otherwise depressed trade market. There are several reasons for their popularity. For breweries, they are a great way to get their beer into drinkers' hands without having to deal with distributors and publicans (though few breweries sell only through their own taprooms). It's great for building a brand, for getting direct feedback on experimental brews and, perhaps crucially, the profit margins in a successful taproom tend to be significantly higher. For drinkers, there is almost a guarantee of the freshest possible beer (an increasingly important factor in the world of craft) served exactly as the brewer would wish it to be served, and even the opportunity to hang out with brewery staff. Although they started off as a kind of glorified serving hatch – only pouring for the public at certain times, with pretty basic facilities – taprooms have evolved into something much more like standards bars, with food, live music and extended opening hours. While the "community pub" has been in decline for decades, taprooms have demonstrated that geography isn't the only way of defining a community. One of the reasons taprooms tend to be such pleasant places for beer lovers is that they attract other beer lovers: a community all of their own.

TERROIR | BEER CULTURE

SEE ALSO
Hops *p119*
Malting *p146*
Spontaneous fermentation
 p208
Water *p231*
Yeast, wild *p245*

The idea that the environment in which something is created gives it a unique, irreplicable character. While this is almost certainly easier to pin down in the wine world, from where the term originates, there are a number of factors that give some beers a decent claim to have their own identifiable terroir.

- Regional malts: these days you can get your hands on pretty much any style of malt you want. However, certain speciality malts are still so closely associated with specific regional styles that to use them for anything else would just be odd.
- Hops: hop varieties tend to be very specific to their country of origin in any case. Moreover, they are extremely sensitive to weather, soil, water and other factors, so that Cascade grown in California will give a very different

character to Cascade grown in Kent.

- Spontaneous fermentation: if any style of beer can lay legitimate claim to having true terroir, it's wild beer. Fermented with wild yeasts and bacteria specific to the precise location in which it's brewed, its character is determined by the surrounding countryside, even the fabric of the brewery building itself. It would be impossible for these beers to be brewed anywhere else.
- Water: while it's true that the mineral makeup of the local water was critical in defining regional styles, modern chemistry and filtration techniques make it easy for brewers to adjust their water source to match any regional profile. The only areas in which it might arguably make a difference are the mineral content of malts and hops as they grow.

TRAPPIST | ORIGIN

In many ways, the monastic brewers of northern Europe can be seen as the forefathers of modern brewing, having transformed it from a casual, often haphazard process into a true craft. In today's beer world, none of these ancient monastic brewers are more revered than the Trappists, an order dating back to France (and an abbey just outside the town of Soligny-la-Trappe) in 1662. A splinter of the Cistercian order, which itself arose from a faction of the even older Benedictines, the Trappists arrived in Belgium in 1802, after being driven out of France during the French Revolution. Settling there, occupying abandoned abbeys and building new ones, the Trappists began a strong culture of agriculture and self-sufficiency that persists to this day, at locations including Orval, Westvleteren, Chimay, Achel, Rochefort and Westmalle.

T
223

Like lambic or champagne, Trappiste is a protected appellation with a strict legal definition: in this case, that Trappist beers must be brewed under the direct supervision of monks at a brewery within the boundaries of a monastery. This definition is so rigorously enforced that several of the larger Trappist breweries are unable to expand any further because they are literally constrained by the boundary walls of the working monasteries they call home. There are currently 11 Trappist breweries around the world, only six of which are in Belgium. While "Trappist" itself is not a style, there are certain styles associated with Trappist and abbey breweries, namely *dubbels*, *tripels* and, to an extent, *saisons*. Abbey beers are often a similar style and quality, but brewed by ordinary businesses, which may or may not have any monastic connection. They don't even really need to be near an abbey.

TRIPEL | STYLE

A strong, punchy golden ale from Belgium, which first emerged around the 1930s but was finally pinned down and popularized by the Trappist monks of Westmalle in the 1950s. A bona fide classic, it's now made by four of Belgium's Trappist breweries, as well as a number of secular abbey breweries, and is a particularly popular export style. Even Belgophile brewers abroad (primarily in the US) have their own *tripels*, some of which are excellent. Character-wise, the *tripel* has much in common with a standard Belgian strong golden ale. It has a deep, burnished golden colour from its base of smooth, clean pilsner malt, which also gives it a soft and rounded malt flavour and aroma. Depending on where it is brewed, there may be other grains in

SEE ALSO
Belgian golden ale *p42*
Belgium *p42*
Esters *p82*
Trappist *p223*
Yeast *p243*

the mix too (light crystal malt, or even oats and wheat in some cases), though these rarely exceed a few percent of the total mash bill. The character may be further lightened by the addition of white sugar, which can contribute up to 20 percent of the total fermentables. Bottle-conditioning is an essential part of the style, contributing a great deal to *tripel*'s distinctive mouthfeel, nuanced flavour and powerful effervescence. Unusually for Belgian beers (and perhaps explaining *tripel*'s popularity in the export market), hops can be quite prominent, with strident herbal and floral aromas, and relatively high bitterness. *Tripels* also exhibit the archetypal Belgian yeast profile, with aggressive spice notes including cinnamon, clove and pepper, and fruity ester characteristics such as apple, pear, peach and banana.

TRUB | BREWING

When wort is transferred to the fermentation vessel, it typically has all sorts of debris still in suspension; this will settle to the bottom over time, while fermentation creates plenty of extra detritus of its own. This collection of dead yeast, hop sediment, tannins, heavy fats and proteins – known as the trub – gathers in the conical base of a modern cylindroconical fermenter and can be removed cleanly and separately from the bright beer. The use of a whirlpool helps this process considerably.

T

UNFILTERED | STYLE

Unfiltered beers, while not a new idea, are definitely becoming more popular as craft beer lovers look for a more "authentic" experience. While it's true there is a noticeable difference when you put filtered and unfiltered versions of the same beer side-by-side – particularly in terms of mouthfeel and, often, flavour – unfiltered beers tend to have a shorter shelf life and should properly be enjoyed fresh.

SEE ALSO
Filtration *p91*
Fining *p92*
Haze *p110*

UNTAPPD | BEER CULTURE

A lot like Ratebeer.com, but aimed squarely at attention-deficient social media types, the Untappd app effectively "gamifies" the serious and scholarly pursuit of beer rating. It allows you to scan barcodes, link up with your friends (and "toast" them, even if they're standing right next to you) and unlock badges, alongside the more pedestrian rating and tasting-notes functionality. It's pretty great.

SEE ALSO
Ratebeer *p183*

U
227

SEE ALSO

Oktoberfest *p162*

VIENNA/MÄRZEN/OKTOBERFEST | STYLE

Three very closely related styles, originating in and around Vienna, that all emerged around the same time, traditionally as a way of using up last autumn's malts and hops (*Märzen* means March, and the idea of brewing a special beer in early spring for this purpose is by no means unique to Germany). These beers are big on malt flavours and aromas, using primarily Munich or Vienna malts, and deliver a hit of biscuity caramel and hints of toast, with barely any hop influence. Although the original Oktoberfest celebration predates the creation of *märzen* by about 30 years, the style quickly became the beer of choice for the festival. In fact, in Germany the term "Oktoberfest" can only be used by brewers in Munich itself.

WASTE WATER | BREWING

There was a time when breweries would just dump their waste water into the nearest river and forget about it. Today, though, particularly larger breweries need to be a little more careful about what they put down the drain, as it tends to be high in sugar and alcohol, low in pH (so quite acidic) and high in temperature. This means a lot of chemistry going down the drain, most notably nutrients, the processing of which puts a lot of strain on the local water-treatment plant. Some larger and more forward-thinking breweries now treat their own effluent before it leaves the brewery. California's Sierra Nevada makes a particular point of only putting water back into the system in as good a state as they received it.

WATER | INGREDIENT

The oft-forgotten fourth ingredient of beer, water typically makes up at least 90 percent of your pint, so is really quite important. Even early brewers understood – before they even knew why – that the qualities of the local water source had a significant impact on the character of the final beer. It's one of the main reasons there is so much regional variation in beer styles, as brewers discovered what worked best for the water in their area, whether it was porter in

W
231

London or Dublin, lager in Munich or pale ale in Burton upon Trent. This is because water isn't just water: it's chock full of minerals picked up from passing through and over rocks on its way to your tap (not to mention any chemicals added by your water provider), which will help or hinder yeast growth, enhance or suppress hop character and have a host of other effects. In reality, then, most modern brewers don't just take their local tap water and use it as is. They add minerals such as limestone, salt, gypsum, zinc and copper to achieve the water "profile" that's most appropriate for the style they're brewing. They may well also filter or otherwise treat their mains water to remove any organic compounds, heavy metals, iron and other trace substances that could spoil the brew. Some large (or particularly meticulous) brewers may even use high-tech reverse-osmosis equipment to strip the water back to a completely neutral state, before adding their choice of minerals.

SEE ALSO
Barley wine *p33*

WEE HEAVY | STYLE

A dark barley wine at the top end of the Scottish ale scale, wee heavy is unashamedly sweet and rich, with a complex, roasty, toffee-laden malt character and only a hint of toasty bitterness to balance it out. Particularly outside of Scotland, you often find this style barrel-aged, where it tends to take on wonderful wine- or sherry-like dried fruit characteristics.

SEE ALSO
Reinheitsgebot p187
Wheat *p236*

WEISSBIER | STYLE

The undisputed champion of summer beers. Served properly, a *weissbier* (white beer) should arrive on the bar in a bullet-shaped bottle, along with a tall, vase-like glass. The bartender will put

the glass over the bottle, invert the whole thing and slowly withdraw the bottle as the glass fills. When almost all the liquid is poured, the bottle is withdrawn and rolled on the bar top to dislodge any yeast sediment and then emptied onto the head already in the glass. Garnish the impressive head with a slice of lemon and you're good to go. *Weissbier* – brewed with 60–70 percent wheat malt – originates in Munich, where a loophole in the *Reinheitsgebot* purity law (there are very few) allows for the use of wheat in *weizens* (wheat beers). *Weissbiers* are definitely best served fresh and not too cold. Their high wheat content gives a creamy mouthfeel and, combined with very high carbonation, produces a magnificent, dense, meringue-like head. Along with pronounced citrus, *weissbier* has a characteristic clove flavour (produced by a special top-fermenting ale yeast) and often banana and other tropical fruit, depending on the brewery.

WEST COAST IPA | STYLE

West Coast US-style IPA deserves its own definition. Although it has its roots in the traditional English IPA – a style of English bitter – it is in reality a very different beast, and its genesis is central to the story of the global craft movement. The West Coast IPA is characterized by the inclusion of powerful whole-cone American hops – notably Cascade, Centennial, Columbus and Chinook – and techniques such as dry-hopping to give layers of complex bitterness and tropical fruit and floral notes, not always balanced by a strong malt presence. The arms race for ever-stronger hop character began in earnest in San Diego in the mid-1990s, with Stone and Ballast Point harnessing new techniques to create high-alcohol, resinous,

235

extremely hoppy IPAs. Love it or hate it, the West Coast style has followed the craft beer movement as it has spread around the world, becoming the signature of our hop-obsessed beer culture.

WHEAT | INGREDIENT

SEE ALSO
Adjunct *p14*
Body *p47*
Esters *p82*
Head *p113*

The very popular wheat beers are something of a German tradition in *dunkelweizen*, *hefeweizen* and *weizenbock*, and in Belgian *witbier* and lambic styles. Wheat is tart, light and refreshing and goes very well with barley. Depending on the style, malted wheat can contribute anything from 5 to 70 percent of the mash bill. The distinctive banana flavours of German wheat beers are driven by the ale yeast used, which creates an ester called isoamyl acetate. The maltier profile of the American *hefeweizen* is less yeast- and more grain-dependent. Unmalted wheat turns up in slightly sharper German beers and the cloudy *witbier*. The hazing is caused by wheat's high-protein content, so expect a thick, foamy head into which you could stick a chocolate flake.

WHIRLPOOL | EQUIPMENT

SEE ALSO
Brewhouse *p55*
Boil *p48*
Boil kettle *p48*
Hot break *p124*
Home-brew *p113*
Trub *p226*
Wort *p240*

Whirlpooling is a common practice at the end of the boil, in which the wort is vigorously stirred in a constant circulating motion to create a vortex in the centre. This creates centripetal force, bringing more dense objects to the centre of the vortex. Because of friction between the wort and the bottom of the vessel, the liquid at the vortex's base moves more slowly, giving it a slightly lower pressure than the liquid near the top. As a result, the trub is pulled into the centre and down, so that when the wort is extracted for cooling, the cloudy trub is left behind. This technique works

for any size of brewery, including home-brew –
after all, the only piece of kit you need to create
an effective whirlpool is a long spoon. Indeed,
on very small kits, where an immersion chiller
is used, a whirlpool can also increase the rate of
chilling, with all the attendant benefits.

WIDGET | EQUIPMENT

The holy grail of bottling and canning has long
been the ability to replicate the characteristics of
draught beer. This is particularly the case with
beers such as Guinness, for which the signature
bar pour is such a central part of the experience.
It led Guinness in the late 1960s to begin
developing a system that would allow draught-
type stout to be poured directly from the can or
bottle. The main challenge of this project was to
replicate the draft system's injection of nitrogen
gas, which gives Guinness its characteristic
small bubbles, thick head and creamy mouthfeel.
The ingenious solution was to include a specially
formed plastic pouch inside the can or bottle,
perforated with tiny holes. When the beer is
opened, the sudden drop in pressure causes
foaming bubbles of nitrogen to erupt from the
pouch, filling the beer and creating an instant
head. The result of this research project is the
somewhat prosaically named "widget". Widgets
are now found in a host of supermarket beers,
including other stouts, porters and bitters. They
are also found in some craft beer cans, such as
Milk Stout Nitro from Colorado's Left Hand
Brewing Co.

W
239

WITBIER | STYLE

Belgium's historically important white beer
traditionally employs a technically tricky

"turbid" mash process to deal with its unusual grain bill, which is a mix of air-dried malt, unmalted wheat and a small quantity of oats. While it's not always brewed this way today, the goal is to produce a wort with lots of starchy carbohydrates and a rich, creamy texture. Another signature of the style was the addition of bitter orange peel and coriander, sometimes augmented with other "secret" spices which varied from brewer to brewer. Northern Europe has been brewing *witbier* in one form or another for almost a millennium, and it is the first beer known to have been hopped. It was almost lost in the mid-20th century, though, and only revived in 1978 with the launch of a beer called Hoegaarden, which has helped repopularize this refreshing summery beer around the world. Its character is unmistakably spicy, with subtle notes of orange, coriander and other spices, along with a creamy mouthfeel and often a touch of tartness.

WORT | BREWING

The malty, sugary solution resulting from mashing and sparging, intended eventually for fermentation; at this point in the process, wort is usually 80–90 percent water, with the remaining 10–20 percent made up of sugars (fermentable and unfermentable), proteins and minerals. Wort remains wort throughout the subsequent boiling (with its addition of hops), cooling and pitching of yeast. It only becomes beer after the yeast has done its work converting the sugar to alcohol. For the amateur brewer, an interesting experiment is to sample the wort at each intermediate stage on its way to the fermentation vessel. It's generally not a particularly tasty experience, but it is informative.

SEE ALSO
Boil *p48*
Fermentation *p85*
Fermentation vessel *p87*
Mash *p151*
Sparge *p207*
Yeast *p243*

"X" | BEER CULTURE

There are several theories as to why the letter X crops up so much in beer naming, from De Ranke's XX bitter to Castlemaine XXXX and even Simonds Archangel XXXXXXX stout. One of the most plausible-sounding explanations is that monastic brewers of yore would stamp a crucifix onto barrels as a guarantee of their provenance and quality, though this sounds a little blasphemous. Another theory suggests that excisemen would mark beers as either strong or weak for tax purposes by chalking one X or two onto the barrel. The symbol could also once have been used to identify "double" beer – where the first wort was reused in a second mash, in theory producing a wort with twice the gravity – with a single X signifying a "single" beer. Or it might just have been because it looks cool.

YARD OF ALE | DRINKING

SEE ALSO
Hangover *p109*

Used in a traditional British drinking game or for special toasts, a yard of ale is a tall beer glass consisting of a long tapered shaft with a bulb at the bottom end. It holds around two pints (about 1.1 litres) of ale, and measures 90cm (3ft or one old British yard) in height. It is customary for the drinker to try to consume the entire contents in one go, though the design of the bulb usually means a good quantity of beer winds up splashing over their face. The US has its own, somewhat less romantic versions of this game: the "beer bong", which essentially involves pouring a can of beer into a funnel and hose, and the "keg stand", in which the drinker is held upside down over a keg and encouraged to drink as much as they can.

YEAST | INGREDIENT

SEE ALSO
Fermentation *p85*
Fermentation temperature
  p86
Pasteur, Louis *p165*
Yeast, wild *p245*
Wort *p240*

This single-celled, eukaryotic fungus has been on Earth for millennia, and is the undisputed star of beer making, responsible for breaking sugar down into carbon dioxide gas and alcohol. These properties make it very useful for baking (carbon dioxide causes bread to rise) and brewing, where yeast transforms the sugary wort into alcoholic beer, with added fizz. Indeed, the word "yeast" comes from the Old English *gist*, meaning "boil", "foam" or "bubble". Although the ancient

Egyptians and Babylonians used yeast in much the same way as we do, the organism itself wasn't observed until 1680, when Dutch polymath Anton van Leeuwenhoek peered down his microscope at its tiny, single cells. In those days, brewers would just have used whatever yeast was around: from plants, in the fermentation vessels or even in the air. By the 1800s, though, the rise in commercial brewing combined with van Leeuwenkoek's discoveries led to the development of the first pure yeast cultures. The pioneering Danish biochemist Emil Christian Hansen, employed by the Carlsberg Laboratory, isolated a particular strain of baker's yeast, *Saccharomyces cerevisiae*, that took a little longer to do its work than most baker's yeasts. Hansen realized this was a positive trait in brewing, as slow fermentation meant fewer off flavours and a greater tolerance to high concentrations of alcohol, allowing brewers to make stronger, better-tasting beer.

The other significant yeast strain isolated around that time was *Saccharomyces pastorianus*, named for its discoverer Louis Pasteur in 1870. The major difference between *S. cerevisiae* and *S. pastorianus* is that the former is classed as a "top-fermenting" yeast because it foams at the top during fermentation, while *S. pastorianus* is "bottom-fermenting" because it doesn't. Top-fermenting yeasts are typically used for brewing ale, while bottom-fermenting yeasts, which thrive at lower temperatures and produce fewer favour-imparting by-products, are used for lagers.

YEAST, BREEDING | SCIENCE

Not all yeasts are created equal, and selecting the best yeast for the style and brewing conditions is vital. The development of new yeasts is an important part of the ongoing evolution of beer,

SEE ALSO
Yeast *p243*

as craft brewers look for new strains that will deliver new characteristics. New yeasts are sometimes identified from wild sources, but are more commonly found lurking among "collections" held by universities, research institutes, businesses and even private microbiologists. The development process typically takes several years and involves isolation of a specific strain, establishing its genetic stability, testing how well it reacts to commercial propagation and then carefully documenting how it performs under real-world brewing conditions. In 1996, *S. cerevisiae* was one of the first organisms to have its entire genome sequenced, heralding a new era of research in which this humble yeast can be manipulated to perform a wide range of tasks outside of brewing.

SEE ALSO
Fermentation *p85*
Lambic *p141*
Spontaneous fermentation
p208
Wort *p240*

YEAST, WILD | INGREDIENT

The yeasts we use in brewing have been carefully isolated and selected over many years for their particular qualities, but countless other distinct species and strains exist in nature, few of which are particularly suited to brewing. These "wild" yeasts are most often found on plants, fruits, skin, soil, insects and in the digestive systems of warm-blooded animals. They are also small and light enough to become airborne. Many brewers experiment with wild yeasts, and they can yield some surprising and delicious (if unpredictable) results. In some cases, such as with lambics, airborne yeast plays a key role in spontaneous fermentation, in which the wort is left open to the environment for extended periods. In other cases, yeast is introduced to the wort directly; brewers looking to experiment with wine yeast, for example, might leave their wort to ferment on a bed of grape skins discarded by a local vineyard.

ZYTHOS | STYLE

A beer brewed for recreational and medicinal purposes in ancient Egypt. Because of its somewhat... odd formulation (set out in the third tractate of the Babylonian Talmud), it acts as both a laxative and an antidiarrhoeal, and is not recommended for anyone who is actually ill. The root of the Ancient Greek word *zythos* and Latin *zythum*, both meaning beer.

INDEX

Page numbers in **bold** refer to main entries

ACKNOWLEDGMENTS

Huge thanks to everyone who's supported me throughout the process of writing this book, including but not limited to the entire team at Octopus, Tilly and Sam (who will hopefully one day find this "Hitchhiker's Guide to Beer" of some practical use), my parents, Lynsey and Lucymarie, Ashley Johnston (the booze world's best and most patient magazine designer), Louise Crane, Team Columbaws, Matthew for keeping me relatively sane and all my friends at Beer52. And special thanks to all the great brewers, writers and beer lovers I get to work with every day, whose combined experience and passion have formed the basis of everything you read here.

An Hachette UK Company
www.hachette.co.uk

First published in Great Britain in 2018 by Mitchell Beazley,
an imprint of Octopus Publishing Group Ltd
Carmelite House
50 Victoria Embankment
London EC4Y 0DZ
www.octopusbooks.co.uk
www.octopusbooksusa.com

Distributed in the US by
Hachette Book Group
1290 Avenue of the Americas
4th and 5th Floors
New York, NY 10104

Distributed in Canada by
Canadian Manda Group
664 Annette St.
Toronto, Ontario, Canada M6S 2C8

ISBN 978-1-78472-388-0

A CIP catalogue record for this book is available from the British Library.

Printed and bound in China

10 9 8 7 6 5 4 3 2 1

Commissioning Editor: Joe Cottington
Creative Director: Jonathan Christie
Illustrator: Jonny Hannah
Junior Editor: Ella Parsons
Copy Editor: Caroline Taggart
Production Controller: Dasha Miller

ABOUT THE AUTHOR

Richard Croasdale is an award-winning journalist, editor-in-chief of *Ferment* craft beer magazine, and an all-round lover of anything cold and hoppy. A member of the Guild of Beer Writers, Richard has travelled the world in search of the best beers and brewers, experiencing the diversity of approaches and cultures that make craft beer so exciting. He lives in Edinburgh, Scotland, and can usually be found evangelizing in the city's many excellent beer and whisky bars.